SNIPPETS FROM A COUNTRY BOY'S MIND

Recollections of Bygone Days

by

Morris Gresham

To Mary Ann & Bill:
I hope this peek inside my brain isn't too scary.
Best regards, my friends,
Morris Gresham

Also by Morris Gresham:

A COUNTRY BOY'S APPETITE
Following Life From One Meal to the Next

COMING UP A COUNTRY BOY
Surviving the '40s and '50s

THEN THE COUNTRY BOY WROTE…
A collection of (mostly) outdoor tales by Morris Gresham

Coming sooner or later:

COMING UP A COUNTRY BOY, THE SEQUEL
Ushering out the 20th Century

One man's opinion:

Memories of the past quite often make me smile, chuckle, laugh or even shed a joyful tear. It's all good. I'm happy I can remember so much. Perhaps the greatest joy is the unexpected, forgotten memories from something said or something read that triggers these treasures.

Morris Gresham's, fourth book, *Snippets From a Country Boy's Mind*, a new book of essays/memories fits the bill. Having lived through the same era as Gresham, under many similar circumstances, his book of memories triggers a treasure trove of memories of my own.

From his childhood escapades, embarrassing moments and life challenges, *Snippets From a Country Boy's Mind* will keep you entertained. Reading Gresham's book is just like having a conversation with the boy. He describes real life in a down home style as only a country boy can. These stories are not sugar coated; he tells them like it was – as he remembers them.

Rodney Nall
Author of:
Laugh Again
Gene and Cecile
Arctic Wilderness Desolation
Serendipity Players...From the Beginning
Big Tex
Fifty One Hundred Word Essays and Thoughts
Senior Readers Theatre, Scripts and Skits
Readers Theatre Hillbilly and More
A Readers Theatre Two Love Stories
A Dukes Mixture...Christmas and More
Senior Living
Favorite Plays

Copyright © 2014 by Morris Gresham

First Edition, February 15, 2015

ALL RIGHTS RESERVED

No part of this book may be reproduced or transmitted in any form or by any means, electronic or mechanical including photocopying, recording, or by any information storage and retrieval system without permission in writing from the Author.

Editorial Consultant – Susie Fluckiger

About the Cover:
    Sunrise Over Buzzard Point ©
    Photo by Morris Gresham

ISBN-10: 150754586X

ISBN-13: 978-1507545867

Printed in the United States of America

ACKNOWLEDGEMENTS

These snippets come from many quarters, some that pop up unbidden, some from one lifetime or another that various individuals recalled to my attention. None helped more than Rodney "Scholar" Nall, a classmate in the Mineral Wells High School Class of 1958. He has brightened so many of my days with that gravelly good morning greeting and his infectious chuckle. If Scholar has a fault, it's that he is disgustingly energetic. He claims to nap a lot, but how could anyone write a book per month and still nap? I want to be just like Scholar when I grow up…

Scholar Nall, 1960   G. Rodney Nall, 2014

DEDICATION

This book is dedicated to my wonderful family: my bride of 53 years, my blood relatives, in-laws, out-laws, nieces, nephews, great nephews, great-nieces and cousins far and near. Collectively, you influenced whatever I am; individually, you are an enduring joy in my life. I love you all.

This is what's left of the Texas segment of Greshams, including the Hamiltons and Pruetts brought into the family by my sisters.
(Photo by Karen Hamilton)

This is a gathering of the Henderson clan before we lost the last three of the original Henderson daughters, Flogene Henderson Thomas, Francis Henderson and Dorothy Henderson Priddy.
(Photo by Lynn Walden)

FOREWORD

After a run-in with a reader, Mark Twain reportedly said, "Last week I wrote that this woman was the ugliest woman I had ever seen. I have since been visited by her sister, and wish to retract my previous statement."

And now I should probably make a similar correction. Not that I have anything bad to say about Morris Gresham's previous books, and not that any of them have been ugly, but I may have insinuated, in a comment in one or another of them, that that particular book was the best walk down memory lane I'd ever read. After reviewing the tome you now hold, I wish to retract my previous insinuation.

As they get older, many people feel a need to write an autobiography. Some of these are fairly interesting, but most could be condensed by Reader's Digest to a tenth of the original length without damage. Indeed, with many, the result would be greatly improved.

Although Morris's previous literary efforts have been enjoyable and entertaining, this latest collection of random neural firings was like an NFL highlight reel – it offered a lot of fun excerpts from Morris's life, without all the boring extraneous details.

Not that Morris is a boring fellow, but nobody's life is fun all the time, not even mine. Morris is no different, but when you get to be Morris's age, whatever age that happens to be, you can look back and pick out a lot of the best parts and have enough for a decent diatribe. That's what Morris did, here, and I like it.

Of course, it helps that I can identify somewhat. As a kid I memorized books when my mom read them to me, and then I'd say the words and turn the pages at the right times, and Mom thought I was reading. When I went to school, and was faced with new material, I was caught out and sent to a remedial reading class. And when I finally actually learned to read, my whole world erupted.

Morris wanted that eruption, and his reply to his mom after his first day of school is the kind of thing I used to say to my mom. The story is in here, so I won't reveal what he said. I will only comment that it is an epic example of Morrisness, the kind of thing I've come to expect from my old, literary friend.

Chances are you will see yourself in some of these stories, as I do. Morris is not some famous, untouchable celebrity, after all, but a regular person, like you and me. And that comes through in his prose, and makes it more fun for the rest of us. What happened to him could have happened to us. Maybe it did.

So enjoy some highlights from a life well lived. I hope you like these stories as much as I did. Just don't be surprised if they sound just a little bit familiar. We all have a highlight reel. We just don't all have the talent to share it with others.

Luckily, Morris does.

Kendal Hemphill
Memphis, Tennessee
10 January 2015
Outdoor humor columnist and public speaker
Book author: ***The Buck Never Got Here***

TABLE OF CONTENTS

Introduction……………………….. p. 14

No Fear………………………………. p. 16

Are You Related to Grits?................ p. 18

Honky Tonk Music………………... p. 20

To Read or Not to Read…………… p. 22

Your Mama………………………… p. 24

The Dangerous Necktie…………… p. 26

Kind Words………………………… p. 28

Noises in the Night………………… p. 32

A Seminar Scare……………………p. 34

Temperance was my Downfall……. p. 36

Appearance is a State of Mind…….. p. 38

Boogers in the Night………………... p. 42

Be Careful Where You Drink……… p. 44

Meeting my Heroes………………… p. 46

How Y'all Are? ……………………. p. 48

It Didn't Take Much………………... p. 52

Triggering Memories……………… p. 56

I Don't Like Thieves………………… p. 58

Secrets That Ain't…………………… p. 60

TABLE OF CONTENTS CONT'D

Messing With Folks……………..…… p. 62

Pros and Cons of Old Age……………. p. 64

God Knows I Cuss……………………. p. 68

The Ultimate Celebration……………. p. 72

It Took an Act of Congress………..… p. 74

Happy Halloween……………………. p. 76

Chicken Bud…………………………. p. 78

What's in a Name……………………. p. 82

Reputations Can be Deceiving………. p. 86

Shootin' at the Law…………………... p. 90

The World was our Playground……... p. 94

I've Earned the Right………………… p. 96

Death Valley, Texas…………………... p. 98

Engage Brain, Open Mouth………..… p. 100

Childless With Kids………………….. p. 104

Competitive Gardening………………. p. 108

Critters are Fun to Watch……………. p. 112

Sometimes the Plan Fails……………... p. 116

No Dogs in the House………………… p. 118

Jokes in Their Genes………………….. p. 122

TABLE OF CONTENTS CONT'D

Beyond Your Front Yard……………….. p. 126

More Than One Boss Bitch……..……. p. 128

No More Mr. America Competitions… p. 132

Letter vs. E-Mails……………………… p. 136

What if it Stops? ……………………… p. 142

Five Foot Eighteen……………………...... p. 144

Some VIPs are Important, Some Ain't.. p. 146

From the Frying Pan into the Fire……. p. 150

It Ain't Fake……………………………. p. 154

Gastronomic Revelations………………. p. 156

Delusions of Grandeur………………… p. 160

Pay It Forward………………………….. p. 164

Where Were You When…………………. p. 168

I Owe You, Ralph…………………….. p. 174

Youth is Wasted on the Young…………. p. 178

Wake Up, America……………………… p. 180

INTRODUCTION

I've always said that, given only one option, I'd rather be lucky than good. A man who is good at what he does might still starve without a little luck. A look under downtown bridges will turn up more good people than lucky ones. That's why I feel so blessed today. I've already had a wonderful life that just keeps getting better and I thank God that He gave me enough sense to recognize my good fortune.

Despite all my blessings, I selfishly ask for more, sending up one prayer with some regularity: that He not allow my body to outlive my brain. Although opinions vary, He has done that; more importantly, God has allowed my sometimes forgetful brain to recall vignettes from long ago, some on purpose, others that simply pop up unbidden. So, in keeping with the Country Boy theme in all my books, we titled this one *Snippets From a Country Boy's Mind*.

When I consulted my *American Heritage Dictionary* to make sure I'd used the word correctly, I found snippet to be quite correct … "*n.* 1. A tidbit or morsel." But then I saw definition "2. *Informal.* A small or mischievous person." It appears I was accidentally correct on both counts. These essays are indeed tidbits or morsels pulled from the recesses of my brain and BS (Baby Sister) insists I'm crazy. Isn't craziness similar to mischievous?

After working off and on for two years on my fourth book and only half finishing it, I complained to old friend Rodney Nall that sorting through all my notes was taking too long, that I couldn't focus my interest long enough to finish it. And I suspected that readers might have the same reaction. Then Rodney suggested I forget organizing it, that I publish a book of stand-alone essays – one subject per short essay. If the subject was interesting enough, there was no need to connect it to similar subjects. What a concept! There was a reason we called him Scholar in Mineral Wells High School!

So, here it is, a collection you can blame on Scholar – unless you like it, in which case I'll take the credit. I took Scholar's advice and wrote randomly as topics came to mind. Hopefully, there is something here to suit everybody; I've included amusing stories, angry tirades, tender thoughts, 70-year-old reminiscences and essays on life as I view it. There's nothing earthshattering here, but if I can get one of you to laugh, or get mad enough to call your congressman, or shed a tear when reminded of your own snippets, then my undertaking is a success. You won't need a bookmark for this one; just breeze through a story, drop it back into the basket and open it at another spot next time.

I suspect that Scholar, and maybe others, will keep his copy in his main library, that little room with porcelain furniture just past the double vanity. I would consider that an honor. One of my favorite Sam Caldwell prints hangs above my porcelain chair and I think of old Sam several times a day – every time I face that Artist's Proof of *Big Mouth & Bud; Lake Livingston.*

Morris Gresham

NO FEAR

When a person is asked about the most important moment in his life, he usually hesitates before naming one. It's a difficult choice, sometimes. I, for one, had several things reach the top spot. The first most important moment, of course, was my birth, but I can't remember the details, so it doesn't count.

The next most important event was the second one, but I remember it, so that moves it right on up to number one. That was the day I accepted Jesus Christ as my Savior. I think most Christians identify that as their most important moment. It might not have seemed important during previous years, but it darned sure becomes the most important thing to them for the rest of eternity. That's why it ranks number one.

But what is your second most important moment? For me, it happened early in the morning of January 23, 1978. I coughed deeply just before the alarm went off and, during my shower, a pain began growing in my chest. I woke up my bride and told her she should get dressed because something was wrong with me. By then I had discomfort in my right arm. I know it's the left arm you've got to worry about, but what if my heart didn't know the difference?

We went into the kitchen and by the time I drank half a cup of coffee, the chest pain worsened and I strained a bit to draw a deep breath. Soon I sat in the unfamiliar passenger seat as Bettie navigated streets which still had scattered ice patches from a recent ice storm. We headed for Oak Cliff Medical and Surgical Hospital, the nearby clinic where our doctors practiced.

I remember thinking that it was probably a heart attack and that I might die. But what I remember most is that moment when I realized that I WASN'T SCARED! Aren't folks supposed to be frightened of dying? I wasn't. I knew where I was going if I died and I felt a marvelous peace filter throughout my body. It was similar to the feeling caused when a pre-surgery happy shot first reaches your bloodstream. I simply relaxed completely and waited to meet either my doctors or my Savior, but without worry.

When we'd parked and entered at the emergency entrance, a young man there immediately lay me down for a chest X-ray while they charted the necessary information, then sent me in a wheelchair up to the Critical Care Unit. We were still chatting in my private room when the phone rang. The nurse immediately began talking excitedly into the phone and barked something to other personnel in the area. Then someone quickly stripped off my shirt; someone else took off my pants; suddenly, as I lay in bed, they tugged hospital scrubs onto my bare body. Everyone talked loudly and at one time as they wheeled equipment into the room.

Suddenly I was terrified! I wasn't afraid of dying, but I was really scared about what they might do to me. The thought flitted through my mind, "Kill me, but don't hurt me!" Dr. Sellman came in to tell me I had a pneumothorax; my right lung had totally collapsed. Then he picked up an instrument that looked like a miniature of one I had watched my father punch through the sides of bloated cows to release gas.

The doctor inserted this instrument between two of my ribs and pulled out the center stem just like Dad did with the cow. But then the doctor slid plastic tubing through the center of the instrument; next he pulled the instrument out of my chest sliding it over the tubing, leaving the tubing in place in my chest. They hooked a vacuum pump to the tubing to pump air out of my chest for five days, giving the hole (wherever it was) time to heal. Finally, they pulled out the tube, taped over the hole and watched me for an hour. When an X-ray showed that the cold patch was holding, they sent me home, good as new... no big deal.

However, I left there knowing two important things: 1.) I do not fear death, and 2.) doctors scare hell out of me.

ARE YOU RELATED TO GRITS?

Before I'd sold a handful of stories, folks began to ask me, "Are you related to Grits?" The question never surprised me since Grits Gresham was the most recognizable outdoorsman in the world at the time. Not only did he appear on Sunday afternoons in *The American Sportsman* on national TV back when folks were allowed to catch fish and shoot critters on network TV, his distinctive western hat and bushy sideburns showed up several time every day in Miller Lite commercials. Since our names are spelled and pronounced identically, it was a natural question.

The answer was no. I'd never met Grits or his son Tom at that time, but I remember one issue of *Bassmaster Magazine* that boasted two articles with my by-line, an article and a column by Grits and an article by Tom. I'm sure bass fishermen of that era suspected a family-run publication – if they noticed the by-lines, that is.

Fast forward to a late '80s Annual Meeting of the Outdoor Writers Association of America, the one in Kalispel, Montana. Everybody was there, including Tom Gresham, a fine writer from Louisiana who later took the reins from his late father to become a radio and TV personality. As I sat at a table for one of our group luncheons, a laughing Wade Bourne of Tennessee and Tom Gresham took the seats on the other side of the table.

Bourne could hardly talk without laughing, but he finally got the story told. A lady at one of the sponsors' tents had looked at Tom's nametag and said, "Are you related to…." Both Tom and Wade knew what was coming next. After all, Tom had been answering the same question for years, until she finished the question with, "…Morris Gresham?" That was a first! Tom was an accomplished professional writer before I ever sat down at my first typewriter, but I was the Gresham she knew. Bourne had a case of giggles all day long.

It turns out the lady had met me at a knife manufacturer's hospitality suite the night before. She didn't know me, Tom or Grits or anyone else in the writing community, but she remembered the fellow who had tried to answer all her questions as a newcomer.

Shortly after that I saw Grits at an American Fishing Tackle Manufacturer's Association meeting, the St. Louis AFTMA Show. We bumped into each other on our way to the President's Reception, a meet and greet affair for VIPs and outdoor writers – I obviously fell into the latter category, Grits was both. We visited as we walked down the long hallway and caught up on news since I'd seen him last, much of it about the Dallas Gun Club. I was a member of the club and he knew many of my friends from the days he had shot live pigeons there.

When we reached the entrance to the reception, we each dutifully filled out our nametags and slapped them on above our shirt pockets. The young man at the table said, "Oh, I'm glad to see you together. I've always wondered if you were related."

So, the rugged old gentleman who was older than my father put an arm around my shoulder and said, "Yes, this is my fawtha."

That earned a hearty laugh, so the half-dozen other times we heard the question during the reception, Grits used the same answer. I got even with him, though; every time anyone asked me if I was related to Grits after that night, I always answered, "Yes, but Grits is from the black sheep side of the family."

It was a joke, Tom....

HONKY TONK MUSIC

My bride and I finally gave up honky-tonks years after the sound got so loud that there were no tables far enough back to prevent headaches. We never gave up listening to the honky-tonk music, though, as long as we had control of the volume knob. Then, as our chosen genre tilted precariously toward hard rock, we found ourselves listening to traditional country. It was sometimes called classic country, or maybe golden country. My favorite CDs include songs by George Strait, Jim Reeves, George Jones, Connie Smith, Loretta Lynn and Faron Young, to name a few.

Imagine our delight when we discovered RFD-TV on satellite TV a few years ago. The network boasts a wide variety of programming of interest to country boys, everything from classic tractor shows to horse training demonstrations to Porter Wagoner re-runs to Country Family Reunion, a program which brings groups of old country performers together to share wonderful stories of the old days interspersed with songs by the original artists. Just a couple of nights ago, we watched performances by Patti Page, Jack Greene, Johnny Russell and B.J Thomas. Great stuff!

I can't help it; I've loved country music all my life. It matters little to me which style I hear, whether it's a country singer, a bluegrass band or a southern gospel quartet, I can happily sing along with any of them – as long as others within hearing distance don't object too loudly.

The colorful stars of the '50s, '60s and '70s were noted for having fun with each other. They didn't travel the nation alone in huge personal busses. Instead, they often rode together in one station wagon with their instruments tied to the roof. That closeness resulted in the birth of legends, giants who sometimes consumed prodigious amounts of alcohol, but rarely touched the scourge of our nation today, that stuff known as recreational drugs. We just called it dope in my day. And it took a dope to use the stuff.

On a recent episode of Country Family Reunion a singer asked Little Jimmy Dickens if it was true that he had bought his wife a treadmill for Christmas. The diminutive country star, who was nearing 90 at the time, admitted that he had, but he claimed it didn't have anything to do with weight loss. "I just wanted to hear her breathe hard again," he explained.

The late Johnny Russell told of a young singer complaining that the old folks had more fun than the younger entertainers. "Well, hell, y'all don't ever do nothin'!" Russell told him. Also, Russell's contemporaries sang their songs rather than screaming and breaking guitars. Does anyone else wonder how music executives can watch every song George Strait sings go to number one and then not promote new crooners of the same mold? Come to think of it, Alan Jackson doesn't do badly with his old-time, smooth style either.

That brings me back to honky tonks. During my prime, we did more romantic buckle polishing than grape stomping, but the last dance hall I entered, you couldn't have heard a siren go off. And all I could see was bodies bobbing like chickens with lopped-off heads. I guess it was dancin', but if that's romantic, I'll never have enough energy again for romance....

TO READ OR NOT TO READ, THAT IS THE QUESTION

The ability to learn by viewing nature firsthand was merely one of the advantages of growing up a country boy. A lack of time to devote to book learning was one of the disadvantages. Oh, Mother spent a lot of time on a pallet with me at naptime reading from Uncle Wiggly books or from one of my rapidly growing collection of comic books, but a country mother's day in the 1940s included a multitude of chores complicated by a total lack of modern conveniences.

For example, the cook stove had to be fed a regular diet of wood, as did the fire under the old iron pot that heated her wash water. Mother also served as the washer agitator, often on a steel rubboard. She also resorted to a manual wringer (two twisting hands) before hanging the clothes on wire clotheslines. The hours required to cook three meals a day for her little family further reduced her teaching time.

I loved the time Mother spent reading to me, but I was frantic to learn to read for myself. Then I could read my books anytime I wanted to instead of depending on the pictures to tell the story. Even comic books had words I needed to know! Luckily, country kids of that era, at least the ones in the Lipan Independent School District, could visit classes before they started to school …a precursor to the kindergarten of later eras, I suppose. Anyway, nearby neighbor Ardith Rose Wilson agreed to be responsible for me (not a small task for a girl only a year older than me) so the bus driver stopped one fine day in 1945 for this excited five-year-old.

Grammar school at that time consisted of two classes per room, first and second grades in one room, third and fourth grades in another room and so on. One grade would study while the teacher taught the other grade, then every hour the grades would swap roles. Since I wasn't a student yet, I sat in Edna Starnes' room at the same desk with Ardith Rose and listened to the lectures for both grades, getting a double dose of learning … in spite of all the attention (and giggles) a little, freckle-faced boy elicited from the older girls. Mrs. Starnes must have been a saint. I remember her as one at any rate.

The day went fairly well; I didn't get into any trouble, didn't run away or get lost or anything drastic. I was a little crestfallen, though, when I got off the bus at the front gate where my mother was waiting. Our conversation that day remained one of her favorite stories she told for forty years or so. "What's wrong?" my discerning mother asked. "I've been to school all day long and I still can't read," I complained.

I must have been born impatient; then it got worse....

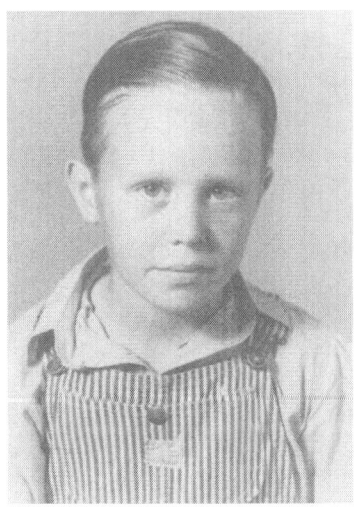

Already a freckle-faced reader by age seven,
thanks to Edna Starnes

YOUR MAMA

One good thing about getting older is the increased say-so you get at your place of employment. And one bad thing is the increased say-so you get at your place of employment. Quite obviously, one knows more about what he's doing after he's grown a few gray hairs, but management often promotes a fellow to a position beyond that to which he aspired.

Yep, they did. If ol' Billy Davis hadn't had that unscheduled stroke, I'd have been happy to do his bidding for many more years. He was a good leader and a good friend who led without being a dictator. Unfortunately, with Billy unable to return to work, my bosses decided that I was his heir apparent.

Damn!

It took months of scavenging through Billy's records and notes to determine exactly what he had in mind. Sadly, Billy had a great memory, but the stroke wiped that all out, including the things he'd never written down. I was determined to avoid the same mistake. I made a physical note of every decision, complaint, mistake or breakthrough. I also made sure that I always had a right hand man who knew my plans and who helped formulate those plans.

I had been perfectly happy designing mechanical gadgetry without the aggravation of supervising younger employees and, worst of all, writing employee evaluations. Most accepted the process and agreed with my astute judgments. Others didn't. Those, I don't want to talk about.

I've known supervisors who led by intimidation, but none of them had ever been my choice as Supervisor of the Year. Nope, my choices were the ones who didn't see supervisor/employee interactions as adversarial relationships. Like them, I was pretty sure that happy employees would be more productive than unhappy ones. Besides, they were more fun to be around. Therefore, the atmosphere in any engineering group I ever led was light and cheery ... well, most of the time. Occasionally, someone might get a little testy from overly-strong teasing, but we always got over it.

For example, when I turned 50, most of my lads were in their early- to mid-30s. This age difference led to frequent references to my age-related defects. I was at one time or another, older than dirt, old as rocks and probably helped Moses engrave the tablets on the mount. And I probably fed Noah's family with fish I caught off the stern of the ark.

Now, 24 years later, I still remember the day one youngster told me, "You're old enough to be my daddy."

I put on as studious a look as possible and, after a few seconds, thoughtfully replied, "You know, I might be. What's your mama's name?"

His face got so red at the ensuing laughter that I regretted the statement … for a couple of seconds. My response, however, did reduce age remarks, true or not….

THE DANGEROUS NECKTIE

During a previous life as a mechanical design engineer, I toiled on contracts for various agencies of the U.S. Department of Defense, including Air Force, Army Ordinance, Army Signal Corps, Navy and Coast Guard. For the benefit of persons unfamiliar with government contracts, it usually pays well, but specific requirements are sometimes ridiculous. Government contractors understand how hammers can cost $500 and a toilet seat might command a comparable price. Believe me, if DoD wrote all the specs, the items would cost just as much at Home Depot or Lowe's. Hell, we might as well let 'em control our health care...

Government agencies often place ridiculous restrictions on contractors, such things as using materials that are more expensive while being inferior at the same time. They also require extensive testing, including destruction of test models at times. That costs money, right? One of the most costly actions, though, involves progress reports. It wouldn't be so bad if it was just a report, but it usually requires what industry calls a dog and pony show.

We'd have numerous employees tied up for weeks writing reports, producing art work and preparing thick manuals for each dignitary attending the progress meetings. It had nothing to do with doing the design. We merely explained the design. They'd send colonels, captains, admirals and other commissioned officers who frequently asked questions that showed a significant lack of knowledge about equipment they were supposed to be overseeing.

It got hectic at times.

I never liked dog and pony shows because I hated to take all that time standing at a screen explaining my designs to big mukedy mucks when it could all have been handled by sending the reports to engineers who knew what they were doing. But, good employee that I was, I'd wear a coat and tie and sit in meetings for several days, making presentations and watching other presentations in case they had any questions for my department.

During one particularly difficult contract, I had a young man under my supervision who was a college co-op student. He was a particularly bright engineering major working for our company prior to his senior year. We gave him a bit of grief for being from New York City, but the 4.0 student always held his own during the bull sessions at break times with quick retorts. When I came out of one of the sessions and took the time to harass him a bit about an engineering drawing on his desk, he was ready for me.

"I'll be glad when these meetings are over," he said.

"Why?" I asked. "You don't have to attend any of them."

"Yeah, but when **you** wear a tie, it cuts off the flow of blood to your brain."

Case closed….

KIND WORDS

After selling words pulled from my mind and assembled into stories for forty years, I realize that most people never notice the byline. They might remember my words of wisdom, but not my name. I discovered this fact some 20 years ago when I bumped into my first cousin at a skeet shoot. He said that my mom had told him I was writing magazine articles. I said, "Yeah, I am. In fact, I wrote an article about a couple of trap shooters in your gun club, Mike Fisher and a fellow in a wheel chair."

"Did you write that!" he exclaimed. "It's posted on our bulletin board at the club. I read it, but I didn't know you wrote it!"

"Yep," I said, "the author's name is usually right below the title. And if you read your *Skeet Shooting Review*, I write at least one article in every issue."

"Really!"

Yep.

Now, I appreciate kind words as much as anyone. Fan letters always please me, but they don't happen often. The first one I ever got was in response to the first story I ever had rejected. I had submitted a story about worm fishing for bass to *The Texas Fisherman*, but it was returned a few days later by the editor saying they were overstocked with worm fishing manuscripts. Although it had never happened to me before, I didn't think much about it. I merely wrote another cover letter and mailed the manuscript on to *Pro Bass Magazine*.

The editor bought it and published it a month later. A few weeks later he sent me a copy of a letter to the editor from Al Eason, an East Texas fishing writer whose work I had read for many years. His extremely complimentary letter might have had something to do with the many articles that editor bought from me in subsequent years.

Another one which warmed my heart came from the late Sig Badt, a crusty old writer who was a fellow member of the Texas Outdoor Writers Association. Sig sent me a handwritten note of thanks for a story I had written about a mutual friend, Lake o' the Pines fishing guide Billy Bass. I still think kindly of that old codger every time I see that note. And it prompts me to recall good times with him in the field.

That reminds me of another crusty old guy that I met during my coverage of the 1995 World Skeet Shooting Championships. Ernie Provost walked up to me and announced that he had just won the senior veteran 410 world championship, I think it was. He told me between gulping breaths that he had lost 75% of his lung capacity to emphysema, but he could still shoot. I was mightily impressed that he had managed the strength to shoot 550 clay birds that week, much less win a championship and I gave him a good paragraph in the story.

A year later, he walked up to me at the 1996 World Championships and I said, "Hello, Ernie. How you doin'?"

"How do you know my name?" he asked.

"Well, you won the senior veteran championship last year," I answered.

"How in the world did you remember my name from one short conversation a year ago," he marveled.

"Well, I remember interesting people, Ernie."

With that we became good friends and I spoke at length with Provost every year until his health stopped him from attending. After that I resorted to telephone calls to the retired wildlife biologist and college professor. A couple of years after meeting me, Provost asked if I was a member of the Outdoor Writers Association of America. I was. Then he asked if I had attended the Annual Conference in Harrisburg, Pennsylvania. I had. Then he asked if I had seen the presentations of the black bear expert and other wildlife biologists. Yes, again. It turns out that one Ernie Provost was one of those experts! That revelation provided fodder for many conversations.

Asked once how I got my subjects in the magazine to provide all the information I wrote, I said that I just asked questions and wrote down the answers. "Obviously, you're good at asking the right questions, but more importantly, you know how to listen to the answers," Provost responded.

Then, during our last face to face meeting a few years before he passed away, Provost said, "You know what I like most about your writing, Gresham? You are a clever writer. You use the same words everyone else uses, but you arrange them in clever combinations."

That is, without doubt, the highest compliment I ever received, and it came from a brilliant, kind man that I respected and still miss.

RIP, Ernie…

NOISES IN THE NIGHT

Most people, after leaving the noise of college dormitories and military barracks behind, rapidly learn to love quiet conditions, especially in the bedroom. Unlucky renters, of course, might wind up in an apartment without sufficient insulation. I remember a newlywed couple that rented the apartment directly above us at the old Aztec Apartments in Oak Cliff. I really admired the man's stamina, but we had jobs and needed sleep. We moved.

We've had no problems since we bought our first house. Well, OK, my bride claims I snore, but surely she's mistaken; I haven't heard a thing!

If working as an outdoor writer has any downside at all, it would have to be the sound effects in fishing lodges, hunting cabins and tents we share with our peers. I soon learned to carry ear plugs in my travel bag just in case a trip degenerated into room sharing. A couple of times I could have used ear muffs in addition to the skeet quality ear plugs.

On one group trip to Lake Guerrero, Mexico, lodge personnel who had observed the nocturnal talents of San Antonio magazine/radio stalwart, the late Charly McTee, wanted to assign him a separate room, but a full lodge spoiled that plan. So, they assigned Charly a bunk at the opposite end of the large, open dormitory from the rest of us. Unfortunately, with Charly at full volume, it wasn't far enough. Luckily, we got tired enough fighting those Mexican bass that those little half-size bottles of liquid pain killer dulled the sound enough for us to catch some zees.

I fished a lot with the late Bill Allen through the years, but after being burned once, I always opted to sleep in the cabin where Bill wasn't. Bill was good, but he couldn't match a fellow on a deer lease we hunted near Evant, Texas in 1987. We had a large house on the lease with several bedrooms. This fellow parked his trailer about 20 feet from the south end of the house. Several of us were sitting in the kitchen at the opposite end of the house one night when one of our hunters said, "Somebody just drove up in a truck. I didn't think anybody else was coming this weekend."

We walked out of the house and found no truck, no lights and nobody. Then we walked back toward the kitchen and the truck sound cranked up again. We looked around and saw no lights, so we walked through the house, past three closed doors and discovered the culprit. The hunter sleeping outside in the trailer was lucky it wasn't mating season for Peterbilts; his nasal call would have brought in a trophy for sure.

I may not be an expert on the science of snoring, but after years of sharing quarters with world class performers, both professional and amateur, I've learned a thing or ten. I can now, without fear of facing ridicule, report with certainty that the world's foremost snorer is not one of my hairy legged outdoor companions. Last spring we validated speculations we had heard by sharing a hotel room with two beds with the champion, a lady I've mentioned in my other books. You remember BS, don't you? Or Baby Sister to folks who haven't read my books. It took her about 15 minutes to get tuned up that night, but after that it was a non-stop performance. I'll never forget it.

Just last week, BS shared her bed for the night with her four-year-old grandson Micah and her granddaughter Ava, Micah's cousin. Micah's father Levi was asleep on a couch in the living room so he wouldn't wake anyone when he slipped out for an early-morning deer hunt. Just before time for Levi to get up, Micah sleepily wandered into the living room.

"What's the matter, bud?" Levi asked.

"It's too loud in there," Micah complained.

Out of the mouths of babes…

A SEMINAR SCARE

A smart man once said that no matter what you do, timing is everything. You get the idea; don't open a harness factory after Henry Ford begins mass production of automobiles. But you shouldn't be too early either. Timing **IS** everything.

So, I was lucky when I began my writing career at the top of my fishing activity. I was fishing with many knowledgeable bass anglers just as great new fishing reservoirs initiated a bass fishing craze. New lakes, new lures and new anglers caused a corresponding explosion in fishing publications. Then, a story sale to a fishing magazine led to my first job as a magazine editor. The publisher of *Bass Clubber Magazine* offered me additional income from commissions on any subscriptions I might pick up at fishing seminars.

It was pretty easy; I learned from some of the best fishermen in the game so all I had to do was describe how we did it – no matter what methods we used. I talked about worm fishing, top water lures, night fishing, catch and release, and on and on and on. I couldn't go wrong since I always told them what tactics worked for us and why.

Then came the scary night I drove to East Texas to be the after dinner speaker at the Tyler Bass Club Annual Awards Banquet. The program director met me at the door, gave me a copy of the program so I'd know what was happening – and when. He introduced me to a number of club members before approaching a gentleman who needed no introduction. He was John Fox, or the American Angler as he was known on his nationally syndicated TV show of the same name. He was an original inductee of the International Fishing Hall of Fame. Then I learned that Fox was making a short presentation immediately prior to my program.

Oh, great! Schedule a young writer to perform and then bring in a pro's pro for him to follow! Oh, well, I would enjoy a gourmet meal even if my spiel didn't generate any sales. Fox was smooth as silk, as I had expected, during his program – which, understandably was a pitch to promote his *American Angler Magazine*. (As a side note, within a year I made sales of manuscripts, color photos and a cover photo to that same magazine edited by well-known outdoor writer Earl Golding of Waco.)

When my time came, I approached the microphone with some trepidation, but forged on ahead. As usual I carried only one sheet of paper with a few bullet notes on my subject for the night. I never made canned speeches, preferring an off-the-cuff presentation. Nobody likes to be read to, at least I don't. I told my audience, "Since I don't make speeches and therefore have no place to lose, you don't have to wait until the end. If I say something that needs explanation, just ask me. After all, I want to talk about what you want to know."

My topic that night was fishing with small worms, thin 4" models, to cure cold weather doldrums. My friends and I had been having phenomenal success with them and I had sold a couple of stories (unpublished at the time) about our tactics. I had not seen one word in print or seen anything on TV about it, so I was introducing brand new information to those Tyler boys. My data was the leading edge of what turned into a major trend away from "bigger is better" shortly thereafter.

Sure enough, I got the first question about five minutes into my talk. As I began my answer, I watched every head turn toward John Fox. "Oh, no," I thought. "I'm a goner!" Then, as I spoke, Fox smiled, kept looking straight at me and began nodding his head in agreement. I know he felt all the eyes upon him although he never acknowledged them, and that kind man continued silent nods of agreement throughout my hour and a half program. Those anglers surely must have had sore necks from twisting toward Fox all night.

I had feared the veteran's talk would make me look bad by comparison, but he had my back all the way. Fox had his detractors, as all public figures do, but I will always remember him with fondness. He raised my credibility at a time few readers knew me, and I made more than a few coins on Tyler Bass Club subscriptions that night as well. A hot meal and money, too!

Thank you, John Fox.

TEMPERANCE WAS MY DOWNFALL

I got inebriated twice when I was young and dumb. I discovered that I didn't like not being in control of my mind and body and vowed to never get wasted again. I can't even drink to impress anyone because, try as I might, I just cannot like Scotch, the one beverage that seems to impress drinkers who know what they're doing. No, I imbibe because I like the taste of some drinks, but not enough to consider getting goofy.

Of course there was that one incident, the one caused by doctor-induced temperance. It all started when I turned 37, yep, that long ago. I began to have dizzy spells and passed out a couple of times for no apparent reason. So, good old Doc Dombrowski inflicted a glucose tolerance test on me and discovered reactive hypoglycemia. Simply put, that meant when I ingested too much sugar or carbohydrates, my blood sugar dropped and I'd faint and fall in the floor. Come to think of it, it did usually happen after I'd had a big Mexican dinner with lots of beans, rice, tortillas and sopapillas washed down with a couple of mugs of high-octane beer. Hm-m-m-m-m…

Anyhow, the doctors told me to lay off that good stuff and drink only a couple of light beers at one time – and only if I ate a lot of protein with it. I thought, "If I can't have as many as I want, I just won't drink any." And I didn't have a drop of alcohol for over two years. Now, that's temperance right there, I don't care who you are.

Then we attended the 50th wedding anniversary party for Louis and Ruby Kothmann, the German owners of our Hill Country deer lease. It would have been disrespectful not to drink at least a little red wine, right? So, I had two small glasses of red accompanied by plenty of sausage and barbecued brisket – with no ill effects!

Wow! That went so well that I decided to try it three weeks later at our company Christmas party. I'd have two glasses of red wine before the big roast beef dinner, then have two more glasses during the final four hours or so of dancing. Unfortunately, they served the wine in water glasses – you know, the kind with vertical ribs like the ones that held my Grandpa's Garrett Sweet Snuff. Well, 12 to 14 ounces of red wine poured quickly into an out-of-practice stomach was already past the point of good sense. By the time I finished the two other planned glasses, I'd forgotten the plan. My bride claims they counted of my drinks, but she's probably not totally trustworthy when she's irritated. She claims I drank 13 water glasses of red wine that night...

Well, maybe I did. The last thing I remembered was helping the band pack their instruments. I don't remember the trip home. She says I gave her accurate directions about how to get out of the unfamiliar area, but then I had a little accident before I made it to the bathroom. Here again, she has been known to fib when she's angry. All I know is that I only left the bed or the couch all day Sunday to CRAWL to the bathroom and back. I made it to work on Monday, but it was noon before I cared whether I lived or not.

You know there's always one fellow that everyone talks about after a company Christmas party. Well, that year he was me, or vice versa. I had a half dozen or so ladies stop by my desk to tell me what I said during a dance with them. It was always the same boast, "I may be drunk, but I'm mobile." And I was, temporarily. But I learned an important lesson that night: red wine should only be used to launch ships.

Revelers at another Continental Electronics Christmas party: Bettie Gresham, Ralph Steward, Betty Metcalf, Virginia Steward

APPEARANCE IS JUST A STATE OF MIND

I just remembered yet another advantage of old age. How many is that now, two? Or three? Never mind, let's get right to it; the mind is a wondrous thing, even after time has wrought many changes. In fact, some improvements are caused by age. OK, maybe it has more to do with experience than age, but one doesn't happen without the other, does it?

Old timers develop the ability to visualize people at various stages of their lives. The older one gets, of course, the more people he knows – and he has more years available to recall. Most young folks don't seem to understand this and I didn't have that ability forever, much as I'd like to claim it. I must have been in my sixties, at least, when I began to notice grown folks running through my mind as children. I'm not sure whether it happens because old folks just naturally sit around and reminisce more or if there's a cerebral switch that allows us to choose the age level of the people who pop into our minds.

Just in case it's a learned ability, I recommend that every one of you, all seven of my readers, begin a regimen of mental exercises to develop that sense. Just close your eyes and think of your son or daughter when they were years younger. Concentrate until the vision becomes clear in your mind. Now, that wasn't so hard, was it? You can speed the process by spending more time perusing old family photo albums. You remember those, don't you, those folders of photos we collected before the advent of telephone cameras and smart phones.

And if you haven't turned the pages of your high school yearbook recently, you'll find a few faces you might have forgotten since your last look. I don't know if we had as much fun as I remember, but the memories are wonderful, even if magnified by time. Every time I open a *Mineral Wells High School Burro*, I am reminded of happier times. And photos of those classmates gone on ahead remind me that we were blissfully unaware of the tremendous joy and sadness to come.

For example, the late J.R. Burns is always on stage with his guitar when he pops into my mind. And although I see photos regularly on Facebook of a still active 74-year-old Billy Woodruff, the image that comes to my mind is of the tall redhead in a sport coat playing his guitar and wailing good old rock 'n' roll. I can't help it. I know what he looks like today, but he's forever locked into 1958 in my mind. I don't know whether arthritis has slowed his fingers as it has for so many of us, but I'll bet he can still get it done. Voices like his don't go away.

Billy Woodruff Band, circa 1958: l-to-r, Billy Woodruff, Clayton Glover, Roy Burns, J.R. Burns, Jim Pratt, Norris Bailey

Although Tooter Boatman has been gone since the early sixties, a flip of the mental switch projects him on the bandstand at Andy's, our favorite hangout in Strawn. Right behind him stand Charlie

O'Bannon and Clayton Glover. And when I play the Tooter Boatman CD my nephew Craig Hamilton so thoughtfully sent me, I see them in all their rockabilly glory. You can relive the years yourself by closing your eyes and cranking up a few Tooter songs on You Tube. It helps, though, if you remember two-steppin' on that smoky dance floor.

The neatest thing, in my mind, about selective memories is the view I see when my bride of 53 years pops into my head. Now, I see her face every day across the table from me or see her head resting peacefully on her pillow; trust me, I know how old she is and I know what she looks like today. She embodies a different beauty today, but she's pretty to me. And I probably caused every wrinkle. Call me senile, if you like, or maybe Alzheimer's is trying to find a foothold, but when I close my eyes, I see the beautiful girl from September 9, 1961, the day I married her.

I wish this same miracle for each of you.

My bride was nearly as pretty in 1961 as she is today.

BOOGERS IN THE NIGHT

There might be someone who has absolutely no fear, but I've never met him. I doubt that you have, either. Oh, we see the "No Fear" T-shirts particularly favored by competitive athletes, but they don't work. Trust me, everybody's got boogers. We all fear something, even if it's only that someone else will get the last piece of chocolate pie. Fears we laugh about, though, are the ones that make other folks jump and shiver. Our own fears, of course, are not funny.

It's fairly easy to discover a person's fears in a deer camp; it's hard to hide anything from campmates. It's even easier if you share a tent with a scaredy cat. On one lease we had near Menard, Texas, old hunting buddy Larry Pendleton and I invited a new hunter to use the third bunk in my tent trailer. He was a good man around a campfire except ….

The young hunter had a little bit of a snit the morning after his first night with us after discovering a four-inch open hole, some sort of unused vent, through the side of the trailer. He railed at length about how easily spiders, centipedes and even possums could get into the trailer while we were asleep. We smiled and wrote it off as a city boy's fears as we watched him cover the hole with duct tape to keep boogers out of our bedroom.

After we moved to another hunting lease near Evant, Texas, the aforementioned outdoorsman met a bobcat as he walked to his bow blind in pre-dawn darkness. He said the bobcat snarled at him and refused to let him pass, so the hunter, armed only with a bow, kept watch over his shoulder as he backtracked to his ATV and drove back to camp to await daybreak. Now, that's fear!

Having grown up on a farm, I've always been careful to watch for snakes and dangerous critters without letting them hamper my activities too much. We had a couple of hunters on my last deer lease, however, who really, really worried about rattlesnakes, or R-snakes as they called them. It didn't do their blood pressure any good when Junior Britton captured 24 rattlesnakes one April from a den beneath a rock about 100 yards from the center of camp. After that, the duo wore snake boots even in camp in July, topped with snake leggings just in case the boots didn't reach high enough. I was wearing shorts and sandals when I killed the four-foot rattlesnake that took up residence beneath the front porch of my camping trailer. You don't have to fear snakes; just don't put any of your body parts any place you can't see.

Sometimes snakes expose overlooked athletic ability, like the time Mike Walker and I wade fished beside the two-mile bridge one night in the late 1980s. We chose wade fishing because the concrete sides of the bridge were covered with slimy green algae that reached six inches above the water line. We had discovered on previous trips that the footing was just too treacherous; so we waded.

Just before dark that day, Walker stood chest deep in dark Tawakoni water about six feet from algae covered concrete when I shouted a heads-up. "Watch that moccasin coming out of the cattails behind you," I yelled. He turned to see a large snake swimming toward him from just a few feet away… and performed an impossible feat! Walker strolled up that algae-covered concrete like walking up an escalator – wearing chest waders all the while! Believe me, no one can stand on that goo, much less climb it. But he did. And now we know; Walker's got boogers, too.

BE CAREFUL WHERE YOU DRINK

We spent 19 years hunting the Kothmann Ranch just south of the little town of Castell. The Llano River was a major side benefit of the ranch. Anytime we visited the lease between the months of May and October, we wade fished the Llano for black bass, spotted bass and Guadalupe bass. It reminded me of fly fishing in Colorado. From the river crossing in Castell, we'd wade upstream one day and downstream the next, catching good numbers of fish on small spinner baits.

Sometimes we'd drive several miles downstream from Castell to Hog Farm crossing. It earned its name from the wondrously odiferous swine operation on the hill above the crossing. You had to be starving for fish to tolerate the scent of that hog poop, believe me. Perhaps it was my imagination, but sometimes I suspected the odor followed us back to North Texas.

One morning I drove out alone to fish the hog farm. I drove across the hard rock crossing and parked beside the road near the river bank. Before getting out my rod, I walked to the shadows beneath a willow at the water's edge to relieve the pressure of my morning coffee. Then, as I retrieved my rod from the truck, a rickety military-era jeep drove up and a grouchy old rancher with a German accent bailed out and, without warning, told me to get my sorry **s off his property. I replied that game wardens told us we could park there because it was a county road and therefore was public property.

"Well, it's not public property," he yelled, "and if you don't get off my land, I'll shoot your g*&%#m **s off."

Well, I was as argumentative as the next young smart alec – and I did have a rifle **and** a pistol in my truck. I decided, however, that a gun battle, even if I won, would cost me more fishing time for filling out forms at the sheriff's office than it would take to drive to the other side of the river. So, I drove up the road a piece and turned around for the reverse crossing. As I drove past the old grouch, he was filling plastic milk jugs from a quiet little sheltered pool. He glared at me as I passed, but I returned the frown with a big smile.

I'd figured out early on that he was the Kothmann I'd been warned about. The rancher who owned our deer lease told us this old bachelor was a cousin of his who was a little on the weird side. He lived like a hermit, without electricity or plumbing and he hauled his drinking water from the Llano River – and he was notoriously grouchy. It's wonderful when an opponent loses without realizing he lost. And that old boy **did** lose. You see, that little pool where he was dipping his drinking water was the same little pool I'd visited earlier.

I don't know if his water tasted like coffee or squashed ants, but the old grouch's water jugs had to be a bit yellowish. So remember, always be careful where you drink and be nice to everyone in the vicinity of your water supply…

MEETING MY HEROES

We come into this life looking for heroes. Starting with Mom, then Dad, then other family members, best friends, teachers, we spend our subsequent years identifying new heroes. If we're lucky, we even get to meet a few of our significant and/or famous heroes. Thanks primarily to my writing career, I became friends with Bill Ruger, the genius firearms inventor, Homer Circle, probably the most famous fishing writer of all time, and Wayne Mayes, probably the best shotgun shooter in history, to name but a few.

I didn't spend enough time with him to become friends with the most famous one, but I'll never forget my first meeting with him. As editor of the magazine for Texas Black Bass Unlimited, an organization raising funds to build a one-of-a-kind fish hatchery near Athens, Texas, I'd already met Waylon Jennings, Crystal Gale and Charlie Daniels, not heroes to me, but interesting people.

Then Leonard Ranne told me he'd talked the son of one of my heroes into being the keynote speaker at the annual fundraiser. The gentleman headed a local baseball team and was announcing his campaign for political office. When I saw him walking alone among the silent auction items before the program began, I seized the opportunity to speak with him.

"Hello, sir," I said, "I'm the editor of the organization's magazine that sponsors this event."

"Hello," he said.

"I just wanted to tell you how much I admire your father," I told him. "He's the finest man I know, I think, outside of my father."

"Well, thank you," he said. "I appreciate that."

"But I lo-o-o-ove your mother," I smiled.

"So do I," he replied. "She's one of a kind."

"And I hope the fruit didn't fall too far from the tree," I concluded.

"I do, too," he said.

Who would have thought that the son of one of my heroes would defeat one of the most popular governors in history to become governor of Texas and go on from there to serve two terms as President of the United States? Yep, my hero George H.W. Bush's son George W. Bush became another of my heroes.

I have watched people heap more abuse on "W" than anyone in history. It's weird that supporters of two men in particular, his predecessor and his successor, have called "W" dumb while those two make "W" look like Albert Einstein. Neither of them can approach his code of ethics (obviously), much less do it with the grace and absolute honesty of George W. Bush. If you don't believe me, just read his books, especially *41 A Portrait of My Father*.

I'm proud to have such remarkable and deserving heroes as 41 and 43.

HOW Y'ALL ARE?

Bettie Carolyn, my bride of 53+ years has made several notable friends as she accompanied me to various functions, gatherings ranging from writing-related functions to political meetings to engineering parties to hunting camps. Her biggest conquest, though, came when we helped the Muscular Dystrophy Association conduct a fund-raising bass fishing tournament at Sam Rayburn Reservoir in 1977.

After launching all the teams on opening morning, all of us worker bees rushed about finalizing all the plans for the rest of the weekend. Then tournament honcho Dee Levins walked up to Bettie accompanied by the night's entertainment and asked her to accompany him for the rest of the day and fulfill any wishes he might have. Luckily, Justin Wilson's primary wish was for an appreciative audience and we had no problem providing that.

We spent an interesting day chatting with the comedian/TV host/safety engineer. After I'd run some tournament errand or another, it was easy to relocate the pseudo-Cajun. I had only to cock my head to listen for Bettie's laughter and then walk toward the sound. Although Wilson was not born a Cajun, he grew up among them and soon discovered that his Cajun stories kept him in demand for seminars as a safety engineer. And he never lapsed from Cajun patois into his native Louisiana accent a single time that day or during any of our subsequent conversations. The personal stories he told us were always as amusing as his records and live performances.

When he discovered that I was a magazine writer covering the event in addition to my MDA duties, he told us he was a writer, too. He asked for my card and promised to send Bettie a copy of his book. I smiled and thought, "Yeah, sure you will," but gladly gave him my card. Then, surprise! A USPS package four days later proved that Wilson was one entertainer who kept his word. It held a copy of *The Justin Wilson Cook Book* with this inscription:

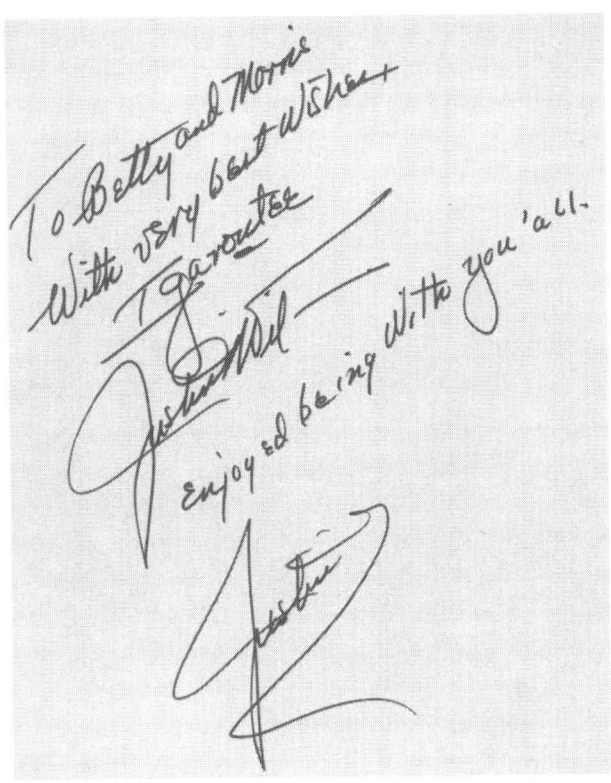

Then, a few days after receiving the book, my phone rang at work and I heard, "Hello dare! How y'all are?"

"I'm fine, Justin, how are you?" I answered.

"How y'all know it was me?" he asked.

I laughed and went on with a chat that would become a fairly steady happening. In fact, if Mike Walker happened to answer our group phone, he'd hand it to me with a simple, "It's Justin."

I'd say, "Hello, Justin."

And he'd invariably ask, "How dey know it was me?"

It seems that every time Justin found himself with a layover at DFW airport, he pulled his business cards to find someone who could entertain him for a few minutes. Once when I asked him what he'd been doing, he answered, "Well, you know I'm a safety engineer and I been here to teach deputy sheriffs how not to shoot they sefs in de foot."

As we met Justin from time to time at other functions, the last of which was the dedication of the Texas River Center in San Marcos, Bettie was always appointed to watch over his famous plantation hat during his performance. He told her he'd had several stolen through the years by fans who really weren't. Well, Bettie never lost his hat once and she was always rewarded with an enthusiastic hug by the big man. We're still sad that we'll never see our late friend again or hear in those melodic tones, "Hello dare! How y'all are?"

Bettie and Justin were in high spirits when we dropped him off at his hotel in San Marcos, the last time we would ever see him.

IT DIDN'T TAKE MUCH

It was called growing up, but my youth could be best described as running unceremoniously through life unable to tell work from fun. It was a busy sharecropper life where everyone had a job. If you finished one chore, the farm would reveal another to take its place. Some of the town folk probably thought we were poor, but we weren't impoverished; we just didn't have any money.

It didn't take much; a huge vegetable garden, a couple of hogs to kill every fall and a calf every couple of years, accompanied by woods full of squirrels, kept us from going hungry. In fact, if you couldn't get fat on farm fare, you'd better just get used to being skinny.

We weren't short of toys, either; we just didn't have much store-bought stuff. A worn-out broom never hit the ground when it was cast aside; it immediately began its reincarnation as Trigger, Scout, Champ or Tony. (Go ahead, name the star who rode Tony. Hint: He always said, "Dig dirt, Tony.") We inevitably recycled old vegetable crates into lots of valuable items: rubber gun stocks, miniature wagons, or maybe a slinger of rocks called a wrist rocket to satisfy political correctness. We made stilts of old bed slats and bailing wire and hand cannons made from a pipe, a pipe cap and a firecracker.

It didn't take much; if you didn't have a "toy" to amuse you, there were plenty of trees around just begging to be climbed. Never one to disappoint any of God's flora, I did my best not to ignore a plea from any tree, regardless of species. Yep, I was a non-denominational climber. And if I tired of the flora, there was always fauna to harass. Animals took the pressure off mailboxes. Shooting squirrels, rabbits or birds was acceptable; damaged mailboxes, on the other hand, always invited appointments with the razor strap. If all else failed, there were always sisters to irritate – and that was never difficult to do.

The only thing about growing up without money is the imprint that remains forever. It's difficult to teach a country boy to spend money freely, whether foolishly or wisely, even after he's climbed well above the poverty line. My investments have always been conservative simply because I remember having no money and I don't ever want to revert to that state. I wouldn't take for any of it, but I don't want to do it again. I wish, though, that everyone could experience lack of money even if just for a little while, because I've noticed that folks who have the least always give the most. There are exceptions of course, but I'll wager that residents of trailer parks give a much larger percentage of income than residents of the million dollar-plus mansions. Oh, rich folks share; it's just that they don't notice it as much as the po' folks. Poor folks know what it's like to have no money so they are quick to help others without any. My Pa used to say, "Give 'til it hurts." And he did.

Thank goodness I found a country girl who grew up under conditions almost identical to mine. When we were dating, our best weekends were those we spent with Jim and Barbara Pratt, our eventual Matron of Honor and Best Man. We'd buy a case of Miller High Life for the weekend and play dominos or cards deep into the night, often until sunup.

After we married, it still didn't take much; we found that money didn't go nearly as far when you were paying all your own bills. For the first few months, small emergencies often left us with only a buck or two at the next payday. But it didn't take much.

Luckily, with a farm-trained girl, no further training was required. She knew that we didn't have to eat ham; we simply doused a can of Spam with Lea & Perrin's, wrapped it and baked it just like the expensive stuff. Despite my physician's warnings, I still like the stuff – Vienna sausages, too.

We were lucky to work at companies that introduced us to lifetime friends, friends we got to know at house parties. There were no admission fees for house parties – and talk is cheap enough. Sometimes we'd get a bunch together and rent a barge to go bream fishing. Over the years we began to invest in deer leases, bass boats and such, but many of our best memories are those that cost little.

Campfires and conversations were some of the most memorable moments of the deer camps; and those were the free parts.

My bride finds her cricket gone as Curtis Costain replaces his bait on our rented barge on Lake o' the Pines. It didn't take much for six of us to enjoy a day on the lake catchin' bluegills.

It brings me to one of my most important beliefs: life is all about people, not stuff. Take away friends and what do you have? Nothing worth talking about, I'd say. I didn't realize it when I was younger and dumber, and I can't remember when the realization hit me that no matter what I do, people are the important part of it. My mother told me once (or more) that if you love people, they'll love you. Maybe, maybe not, but I try.

I even noticed that my writing, after the first two or three articles used up all my personal knowledge, focused more on the people I wrote about than about their skills. The person became the story, not just his ability to catch fish or break targets. I can honestly say that I treasure every friend I've made during my 74 years and every reader I've influenced in any way during the last 40 years.

It didn't take much...

Nope, it didn't take much, just a boat and a pole most of the time...

TRIGGERING MEMORIES

One benefit of reaching the age of 74 (yes, there are a few!) is enjoying the hundreds of thousands little memories that make up your past. And you never know what will trigger one of those memories. One was triggered just last week, for example, as I rode my John Deere lawn tractor to mow the right of way on my back 40 (well, OK, the back 1/2), I saw a three-foot copperhead snake on the edge of the pavement. It was a good copperhead, a dead one. Now, I understand that all of God's creatures have a purpose and a place on this earth ... but not if they slither onto my property.

That three-footer reminded me of a morning back in 1952 when Mom asked me to pull a few sunflowers out of the maize patch before I came back to the house from driving the cows to pasture. A rain the day before should have softened the black dirt enough for a 12-year-old to pull up the sturdy stalks with no problem. And it did, at least for the first couple. When I got to the third one, I planted my bare feet firmly on each side of the stalk and bent to grip the stalk. Then I sensed that something didn't feel quite right. I pulled the leaves aside to discover a copperhead's head barely visible on the inside of my foot while his hindmost parts squirmed on the other side of the same foot.

Then, with absolutely no rehearsal, I initiated what was surely the world record for the standing broad jump. Record or not, it was quick enough and far enough to keep that snake from laying a fang on me. Being an opinionated dude (even at age 12), I wreaked vengeance on that poisonous little critter as soon as I could borrow a sharp hoe from the McClesky family across the road. I found the dummy under the same stalk and quickly cut him into pieces far too small to skin. The pieces would have been even too small for button covers.

That experience kept me wary of copperheads until this day and I'm sure it will continue for however long I remain in command of my brain, or vice versa, as the case may be. Also, I never developed a passion for pulling stalks, sunflower or any other variety. And if trapped into such duty, you can be sure that (1) I wore shoes and (2) I checked the undergrowth carefully for sneaky snakes. Most rattlesnakes give a warning before they strike, but not those sneaky copperheads! Please, God, just let them fulfil their purposes in life far from me!

    Amen….

I DON'T LIKE THIEVES

There we were, having a great time yesterday at my bride's home away from home, the Eldorado Casino in Shreveport, when **BOOM** – all hell broke loose. It began innocently enough with me waiting in a short line at a redemption/change kiosk near the south end of the second floor. Oh, I remember grumbling internally when the nice lady directly in front of me inserted several tickets, one at a time. "Why me?" I wondered briefly before feeling glad for the lady who had done pretty well for herself. She collected a total of $298.

She removed her bills and stepped aside as I cashed my single ticket. I'd collected my bills and moved a couple of steps from the kiosk when I saw the lady pause and look down at a bill at her feet. She was already stooping to retrieve the bill she'd dropped when a Hispanic man quickly snatched the bill off the floor and took quick steps away from the lady. When I saw her startled look as she reached her hand toward her departing money, my instincts took over. I shouted, "HEY!" in a booming voice, getting almost everyone's attention in the casino. I'm pretty sure the departing ne'er do well heard me as well since he shifted into an even faster walk.

Boy, am I glad this guy wasn't an adept thief! He looked like Joe Average except for the light colored baseball cap he wore. If he'd snatched it off his head, I would never have been able to follow him through the crowded casino. But even an arthritic old soul can keep his eye on a cap moving in a steady, but crooked, path toward the exit. I shouted a couple of more times and whistled once to get his attention. When I saw him dart out the exit, I shouted at the security officers there, "Someone stop that guy! He stole a woman's money!" Believe me, that got the officers' attention.

When I huffed and puffed up to them, I pointed and said, "There he is, the guy in the cap!" When he quickly disappeared behind a column and didn't reappear, I yelled, "He's going up the escalator!" An officer took off after him while I limped along at a much slower rate. When I reached the third floor, I asked the guards there if they'd seen a guy in a ball cap just come by, that he had taken some money from a woman. "Oh, him. They already took him back downstairs."

I arrived back at the officers' position to find Security Night Manager Tom Brozik questioning a couple of Hispanics. When the man said he'd only found the money lying on the floor unattended, his female companion said, "He deene do notheen!"

"They're lying!" I shouted. "I saw him take it!"

At that point, Mr. Brozik pointed at me and said, "Stand right over there and be quiet. I'll talk to you after I've heard his side of it."

I took no offense at his request since I'd cast doubt on the runner's claims, exactly what I'd intended. Brozik then listened to my story and asked me to give him a written statement, which I was glad to provide.

By the time I found my way back to my bride, I'd depleted almost all of the adrenaline a 74-year-old body can generate. I told her most of the story and we headed for our room for a little rest. As we neared the exit, I saw the lady, who introduced herself as Sherrye Dotson of Jacksonville, Texas, and asked her if she'd gotten her money back. "Yes," she said, "It was a hundred dollar bill. I can't thank you enough for helping because I could never have found him."

Mr. Brozik walked over and shook my hand, thanking me for stepping up. "It's all done, then?" I asked.

"Yes," he said. "We had your statement, Mrs. Dotson's statement and my officers' observations and they all matched. Now, I'm no mathematician, but three to one is pretty clear so we escorted the gentleman out the door and told him not to return in his lifetime."

"Good!" My bride chimed in. "This is **MY** casino and I don't want people messing around in my casino."

"We don't want him messing around in your casino either," Brozik said, "so you just keep coming. He won't be back."

"Good," I said, "I don't like thieves."

SECRETS THAT AIN'T

During that lifetime I spent in engineering, projects for government entities took up most of the first 29 years. Therefore, every project I worked was classified as confidential at the least and many were secret or top secret, some with stringent conditions that made a country boy shake his head more than once.

For example, I worked for several years on one series of transmitters installed on the air force base of a foreign nation. The big secret was the name of the island where the installation was located. Designating the location as secret is not surprising, but when the company sent dozens of employees to the site over several years, it's hard to believe that the Commies couldn't tail one or the other of us to discover the location… if they really wanted to know. No matter, when I left for my site survey assignment, my wife was told that I traveled to London and Beyond, the same destination all spouses were told.

I became part of another fun secret during the week I worked on the island installation with the project manager. He drove me to a high point of the base the first morning so that I could witness one of the poorest kept secrets of all time, the takeoff of the SR-71 Blackbird, the legendary high altitude spy plane that flew above the USSR every day. What a sight! That humongous machine lumbered down the runway and slowly lifted off the ground. At that point, all slowness ended. It shot upward so rapidly that it became a dot in mere seconds, shaking the very earth as it rose.

We watched it take off a couple of times that week and heard it every morning. They didn't make ear plugs good enough to block the noise. When the program manager and I checked out the last evening with the site commander, he asked me what I thought of &*#@&. I replied that the scenery was fantastic and the food was great, but that the most impressive sight "was that thing that doesn't exist taking off every morning."

Well, you would have thought I'd slapped him in the face with a wet jock strap! "Nothing happened! You saw nothing!" he sputtered.

I smiled and said, "That's what I said, that thing that doesn't exist."

He kept sputtering, but I shut up. I can tell when a fella can't take a joke, especially when the plane rattled every bedroom window in the large city it flew over. I can't believe there wasn't at least one Commie on that island who didn't look up at the noise and say, "Man that' is one big, black bird!" But my project manager said the young officer was really upset by my remark made in his private office. Who knew it was so easy to become a security risk. How was I to know that his office might be bugged? Shame on me!

The last super secret job I was assigned to work, we had to be read onto the job and were warned if we told anyone details of the project, including the name of the agency who awarded us the contract, we would be fined megabucks and spend up to ten years in jail. We signed papers signifying that we understood the rules and the penalties for violating them.

So, after working for months to design the equipment, we prepared to install it in special containers provided by the contracting agency, the agency that we could go to prison for identifying. Well, when the first three containers arrived on the backs of 18-wheelers, several of us got a full-grown case of giggles. You guessed it; the name of that secret agency was painted in huge letters down the sides of all three containers! You know the sad part of the story? I'll bet not a single bureaucrat paid a penny in fines nor did one spend a day in the stockade for spilling the beans.

Sort of makes a person want to let the government to handle his health care, huh?

MESSING WITH FOLKS

Through absolutely no fault of my own, I seem to make a habit of messing with folks. It's not intentional; it's just that any funny thoughts that enter my mind jump right on out there – totally unbidden. All the inhibitions of my quiet youth have been replaced by a recklessness that frequently prompts me to ask, "Did I say that?"

Incidents seem to happen more often in Casinos than anywhere else, although any public place will do. Some folks suspect that the availability of free adult beverages might exert some influence on the frequency, but my bride insists that I'm crazy all the time, whether I'm holding a Negro Modello or not. I think it's caused by my preference for laughter instead of glum faces. In fact, I've been known to harass grumpy folks intentionally until they smile and join the fun. Oh, I'll fail once in a while, but if I do and a person storms off in a huff, he's doomed to be with someone he richly deserves … himself.

I was in fine form one weekend in 2014 and, before the trip was over, I ended up as both the messor and the messee. As my bride and I accompanied BS (Baby Sister) on our first trip to the Treasures of the Eldorado kiosks at the Eldorado Casino in Shreveport, Louisiana, we found the entire display GONE! For years we had swiped our players cards every two hours for all sorts of prizes, ranging from coffee cups to cash awards to extra chances in the $10,000 drawing that afternoon. *Que pasa*?

On my way to the Player's Club to ask about the missing game, I decided (at the exact moment my mouth opened), to mess with the young representative. "Young lady," I said excitedly, "I don't know if anyone has reported this, but you've got a real problem!"

"Really! What's wrong?" she responded.

"Somebody stole all the Treasures of the Eldorado machines!" I breathlessly related.

"Oh, no!" she responded. "All of them?"

"Every last one of them," I confirmed. "That whole end of the floor is empty! How did they get those big things out of there without somebody noticing?"

The young lady obviously had met a lot of old fools because she played right along as the game progressed. The fun part was watching the reaction of other folks to our animated discussion. It turns out that the casino had replaced the long-running promotion in favor of cash giveaways to individuals actively playing slot machines. They obviously gave my $1,000 to somebody else, but that's OK. We had a good time anyway.

Of course, I had messed with a young lady earlier at the hotel check-in desk and discovered upon checkout that she has a good memory for old fools. She scanned Baby Sister's room key and said, "There are no charges, Ms. Pruett. Have a good day." Then she scanned my room key, smiled at me and said, "Your charges come to $229.00, Mr. Gresham. Would you like to leave that on your American Express card?"

In response to my sputtering, and somewhat excited, reminder that it was a comp room, she smiled broadly and said, "Gotcha!"

She earned a hearty laugh from me, since I've always maintained that you'd better be able to take it if you're going to put it out. Just think, after another 50 years or so of aging, that young lady will really be a hoot!

PROS AND CONS OF OLD AGE

Many of my best memories of years past include sitting on the porch listening to one old timer or another tell stories of the old days. Like my Cherokee ancestors, I revere my elders. Then, suddenly I discover one day that **I'm** the elder. Thing is, there are fewer porches to sit on nowadays and not many young'uns interested enough to listen. It doesn't matter a whit, though; memories are worth all the trials of the journey. And I still hang out with folks older than me because, better or worse, they had different experiences and I like hearing about them.

During the early years of my marriage, my bride and I spent many hours listening to stories told by my 80-year-old grandfather. Pa told us about their lives with no electricity or indoor toilets or automobiles. He told one story of holding onto his horse's tail as it swam them across the flooded Brazos River. He told us about the dances at private homes (or barns) and gave us samples of his square dance calling and his buck dancing.

David Solomon Emberlin, left, was my birth grandfather. His brother James Thomas Emberlin, right, reared my mother – and me. Tom was Daddy to Mom and will always be my Pa.

In late summer, the whole Emberlin family climbed into a wagon bound for the cotton fields of West Texas. There, every member of the family, young and old, picked cotton to earn enough money to get them through the following year. They fashioned lean-tos by attaching canvas to the side of the wagon. Some slept in the wagon, some under it and the rest beneath the lean-to. Pa said living in the wagon and cooking over a campfire was similar to a camping vacation, except that picking cotton was never a vacation.

Gordon Hubbard scratches Lightning, the horse that made him the tallest cowboy in every parade. Visits to his house south of Mineral Wells often began with a stop to see his parents, Shug and Blanche.

We spent a lot of our idle time in the sixties and seventies with close friends Jean and Gordon Hubbard who lived south of Mineral Wells. We often arrived at their place early since it gave us an excuse to visit Gordon's mother and father who lived on an adjoining farm. Blanche and Shug Hubbard, in their 80s at the time, also told great stories. Shug told me once about watching my great grandmother ride to the hounds "across those fields over yonder" with her long, auburn hair flowing behind her. She was, he said, "a fine figger of a woman." You could almost hear the hounds baying and hear the thunder of horses' hooves as he told his stories.

Shug was a tall old cowboy who would have made John Wayne proud. He was somewhere close to 20 when he had a disagreement with another cowboy over the affections of a young lady. During the ensuing fight, Shug pistol whipped the other fellow. He hurriedly left Texas thinking he had killed him. He worked as a cowboy in New Mexico, laying low for a couple of years before finally getting word that his opponent hadn't died.

And that was just the beginning of a remarkable life. Shug held jobs which gave him unlimited story data. He was a streetcar conductor in Dallas before becoming part of the Dallas Police Department's first motorcycle squad. In addition to his early cowboying years, Shug also labored in a brickyard, as brick manufacturing plants were called at the time. He kept livestock and operated a small farm about seven miles south of Mineral Wells, spending his adult years with his wife Blanche, a preacher's daughter. He led a remarkable life, really, for a man who had fled the state to avoid prosecution for murder. And he went out like a proper cowboy, collapsing in death while feeding horses in Gordon's corral.

If I'd had a tape recorder in those years, I'd have enough pioneer details to write a library full of books. And that's without mentioning rancher Betty Fambro!

GOD KNOWS I CUSS

I don't know what triggers those special bonds we form with some folks, but probably the swiftest bond we ever formed was with a Breckenridge, Texas family. We met Billy Sam and Betty Fambro when we visited their home in the late 1990s to pick up our hunting permits for the CJ Pasture of the Walker Ranch. That quick visit lasted over three hours while Betty showed us around several rooms of a home that contained more interesting items than a museum of natural history. By the time we left, my bride Bettie had discovered that the Ag teacher at Millsap High School while she was there was Sam's brother Tuffy Fambro – uh, Mr. Fambro, that is.

The stories just kept coming – for the next 15 years. As members of a pioneer ranching family, Sam and Betty lived through exciting times, and Betty remembered every one of them. She allowed mild-mannered Sam to tell a story once in a while, but she was the family historian. All of the Fambros were active in community activities and multiple businesses through the years. Among many other activities, Sam had served as the Mayor of Breckenridge and Chairman of the Stephens Memorial Hospital Board. It would take many pages to list all of their positions and honors.

The tall, handsome man and pretty young lady had noticed each other the first time they saw each other in downtown Breckenridge. Sam asked her that day to be his date for the following night and that date led to their marriage three weeks later. Betty was 17, Sam 19. It was a partnership that lasted 69 years and produced three sons, and a passel of grandchildren and great-grandchildren.

Betty Fambro defined the word colorful. She was proud that she had ridden horses and worked cattle alongside the men during their early ranching years. She claimed she could do a man's work and didn't take any guff off anybody. She said her mother told her "if you call a man a son-of-a-bitch, he knows exactly what you mean."

I asked Betty, a lady with a four-foot blue neon cross in her front yard, how she squared her colorful language with her strong

Christian faith. "God knows I cuss," she answered. "I talk to him about it every night." She was not shy about using her full vocabulary on anyone who broke her hunting rules; Betty handled all the hunters for decades while Sam took care of the cattle ranching – and she didn't need any help.

Until a stroke in her mid-'80s slowed Betty down a bit, she drove that old blue station wagon to all the hunting leases alone, checking hunters, writing permits, chewing butt, whatever was needed. She had to open five gates to get to our 2,000-acre pasture; there's no telling how many more she opened on the rough ranch roads of the remaining 18,000 acres they leased from the Buckner Trust for cattle grazing and hunting for 50-plus years.

Before long, we were visiting Sam and Betty at least once a month, often in the company of Ana and John Echols. We usually had lunch with them, sometimes at their home, sometimes at one of their favorite restaurants. It was a real trick to wrestle a check away from Sam. He told me once, "I like buying lunch for my friends and I'm good at it. Humor me." So we did. Occasionally he'd relent and let someone else buy, but never twice in a row. Never!

Sam was sitting in the breezeway near his "Rancher Crossing" sign when we drove up once. As he struggled to rise from the low chair, I said, "You don't have to get up, Sam."

"Harrumph," he grumbled, "you can't get a hug sitting down."

He meant from the girls, not from me and John – until the last few months of his life. Then we all got hugs from both of them. And Sam always rewarded my bride with a kiss on the cheek. After we lost Sam, Betty suffered bouts of depression, quite understandable when a couple has been married for 69 years. We visited as often as we could after that; her son Sammy said our visits perked her up more than anything else. Reminiscing reminded her of better days and took her mind off our loss for a little while. We always heard new stories as well as some she re-told. It didn't matter, Betty stories deserved re-telling.

Like Sam, Betty's mind remained sharp even as her body failed. When the family called to tell us we'd better not wait if we wanted to talk to her, we immediately headed west. Betty was bedfast and weak that day, but she still didn't mince words. "They all know I'm still the boss," she said. And they did.

We learned one last thing from her that day. "Do you know what I call Joey's wife?" she asked. "Piss ant. That's what I've called her ever since they married."

We're grateful we got to tell Betty we loved her one final time, but I will be forever disappointed that we never got around to putting her memories in print. I should have started tape recording our visits the day she first told me she wanted to write a book. She already had a name picked out – *Them Damned Fambros*.

I'm sure I'll hear about it when we meet again on the other side. She'll probably have Sam shaped up by then.

My bride Bettie and I dropped by for lunch with Betty Fambro a few weeks before she left us. We will always miss her quick wit…
(Photo by Christi Wagner)

Betty and Sam Fambro sit in their Breckenridge kitchen, circa 2005.

THE ULTIMATE CELEBRATION

One unwelcome side effect of senior citizenship is a rapidly increasing number of memorial services one attends. Then, when you reach your mid-seventies, you realize your demise won't upset too many of your friends; many of them are already gone. Just when I thought I'd witnessed everything imaginable in memorial services, I attended the ultimate celebration last week – and it was for a gentleman I'd never met!

I've always maintained that memorial services are for those who remain, not the ones who are gone. And that's what I was doing at the memorial celebration on December 6, 2014, for Dale Melcher Ozment of Hillsboro, Texas, a 79-year-old man I didn't know. I attended to show support and respect for his family, especially for his son Cord Ozment. Cord is such a sincere, likable and quick-witted young man that the picture of his father painted by Rev. Leah Hidde-Gregory, pastor of the First United Methodist Church in Hillsboro, explained the obvious origin of those traits.

The Reverend revealed that witty Dale Ozment, Oz to his friends, continued his influence after his death, leaving strict instructions for his memorial service. His wife Jo Ann Ozment thought the letter he left was surely a joke, but Cord and his sister D'Ann knew it was real. And what he intended was what he'd get.

First, he instructed them to begin the service with *Amazing Grace* played on a harmonica. Dale knew what he was doing; the plaintive notes were as haunting as the trumpet playing *Taps* at a military funeral. Dale's instruction that *Swing Low, Sweet Chariot* be sung *a Capella* from the floor of the chapel was followed perfectly. A young lady performed a spirited, and beautiful, rendition that would have fit right in at a New Orleans homegoing. Rev. Hidde-Gregory and two of Dale's closest friends outlined his life and told marvelous stories of a bright and funny man. Rev. Hidde-Gregory told of visiting him in the hospital near the end; he told her not to worry it was only his warranty expiring.

We heard stories of his love for Oklahoma State University and his beloved Sigma Alpha Epsilon fraternity. They told of his special love for his bride Jo Ann; days before he passed over, he said to Rev. Hidde-Gregory, "She's still pretty, isn't she?" The Reverend apologized to Dale's twin teenage grandsons for not knowing their real names; she knows them only by the nicknames lovingly bestowed by Dale. He called them Peanut and Goober.

We heard stories of Dale's work on offshore drilling platforms, engineering positions and 30 years of sales and management positions in the recreational vehicle industry – his successes always complemented by witty repartee. He was good with his hands and his engineering background enabled him to build anything – woodwork, metal work, whatever … he could, and did, do it all. In addition to his family, Dale loved his dogs which were, after all, family members themselves. He passed this love of dogs on down to Cord.

Just before the end of the service, Rev. Hidde-Gregory announced that Dale obviously had already left the building since it was kickoff time for the OSU football game.

The final instruction Oz left for the service was that all of his friends who attended, all seven of them, join in to sing *Blessed Assurance*. Surely he knew that there would be many more than seven. There were; a packed house sang the ageless hymn. After the benediction, I made my way toward the minister and waited patiently behind a long line of Oz's friends. When I finally took her hand and introduced myself, I asked, "Do you have **any** idea what an awesome thing you just did?"

"Oh, thank you so much," she smiled.

"I never met Dale Ozment," I confessed, "and the service you conducted really makes me sad that I never knew him. All the stories made me realize that I missed knowing a really special person. I thank you for that."

I wish I'd had the opportunity to thank Dale Ozment in person for helping mold Cord into the remarkable individual we know and love, but I can leave a late message like the letter he left for us:

Rest in peace, Dale Ozment, and thank you for all you did...

IT TOOK AN ACT OF CONGRESS

I learned much of what I know about government and politics from my high school American history and civics teacher, Mrs. E.A. "Winnie" Fiedler. Since my association with her ended during the Eisenhower administration, I cannot be sure what her feelings about the actions of executive, legislative and judicial branches of our government would be today. I would wager, however, that the old gal would be horrified today by widespread disregard for the U.S. Constitution. Also, Winnie probably would shake her head in disgust at the spin doctors of today, the guys who explain any action, ANY action, by putting their **spin** on it. In the '50s we called it lying; today they call it spinning. What was lying in those days is just politics as usual today.

I became more interested in politics in the early 1990s due to my employment at the government-funded Superconducting Super Collider. Although most folks today have forgotten that monumental scientific program, those who were ever aware of it, it was widely supported by the legislators of almost every state ... until Texas was picked as the location for the project.

Although the project began well before George H.W. Bush's election, the Texas bashing grew to a crescendo during his term. Hardly a week passed without numerous rants in newspapers, on radio and T.V. and on the floor of both houses of Congress. California leaders opposed it as too expensive, as did New York Senator Charles Schumer. He led the charge to cancel the project because it was running over budget.

Oddly enough, the SSC was designed and headed by the same scientists who built the Fermi National Accelerator and Laboratory (Fermilab), America's premier particle physics laboratory located in Illinois. When the top Fermilab/SSC scientist left just a few months after my arrival, scientists said that they never would have completed Fermilab under the same requirements DoE imposed on the SSC.

The most obvious problem was a lack of any other projects to amuse the Department of Energy. With no nuclear reactors or similar projects on the horizon, your friendly government, instead of sending employees home as any business would when they become overstaffed, sent them all to the SSC.

And what do you think all those DoE employees did? Each of them asked for reports and meetings without end. Instead of designing equipment, every SSC employee spent much of their time answering questions for government overseers. These same DoE managers asked SSC managers why they were running behind schedule and over budget. Duh-h-h-h-h...

When Bill Clinton defeated Bush 41's reelection bid, no one was surprised when Schumer began calling for cancellation of the project. By this time, the Linear accelerator was complete and the 54-mile accelerator tunnel some 200 feet underground was half finished. One thing Chuckie Schumer forgot to tell U.S. citizens was that 48 states had major contracts for the project, as did several foreign partners. They didn't just bash Texas; they bashed everybody!

Of course, Clinton's refusal to support the SSC led to its immediate cancellation. Mr. Schumer's delighted rants in the Senate and on television sounded exactly like the brays of his party's symbol. When he told voters how much money he saved the country, though, he forgot to tell them that it cost more to close the project that it would have cost to complete it. That is a fact that any fifth grader can corroborate by checking public financial records. The difference is that taxpayers bore the cost and got nothing in exchange. Without Schumer, we still would have paid, but we would have been the proud owners of the finest scientific laboratory in the world. Instead, we send our scientists overseas to work today and continue to buy almost all of our radioisotopes from foreign sources.

I hope Mr. Schumer and Mr. Clinton are proud of what they cost U.S. citizens and the world. As for me, I can proudly say, "It took an act of Congress to fire me."

HAPPY HALLOWEEN

We discover some neat stories by sheer accident, such as one a young lady shared with me on a return flight from a mid-'70s Shooting, Hunting and Outdoor Trade Show in Las Vegas. After discussing experiences we'd had at the SHOT Show, we talked about my engineering duties and her job as a court reporter in Dallas. I'll never forget her most memorable experience in a courtroom…

The story began when an outbreak of violent armed robberies prompted police to form shotgun squads in the late 1960s. It wasn't a secret program; newspapers, radio and TV reported that hidden officers armed with shotguns would shoot any armed robbers who entered the store and refused to surrender. It didn't work all that well as a preventative measure, but it surely rid the city of 11 armed robbers in a short period of time. Some others even survived the experience. My new court reporter friend remembered working the trial of one of those survivors.

The defense insisted that the officers hadn't identified themselves properly as police. The officer who'd shot the armed robber testified that he had indeed identified himself to the robber dressed in a Halloween costume with his face covered by a full plastic mask. The defendant's testimony indicated that his attorney probably hadn't coached him much about what to say. When the defense attorney asked if the officer had identified himself, the defendant said, "Naw, suh, he sho' didn't. He jus' hollered 'Happy Halloween, Mo#&*#F*$&er!' And then he shot me!"

Luckily, most juries of that era believed persons armed with firearms robbing store clerks deserved to be shot. Accordingly, survivors spent time in prison. The program took a lot of armed criminals off the street and probably saved the lives of countless innocent people. Unfortunately, political activists decided the program wasn't fair to non-whites because most of the criminals caught or shot were not white. They discounted any idea that non-whites might be robbing more stores than whites did. Police were obviously targeting non-whites. So, idiocy reigned and shotgun squads were discontinued, making life much more dangerous for storekeepers. And guess what? A large percentage of the storekeeper killers today are non-white! Duh-h-h-h.

I saw some of those same clueless activists on TV just this week demonstrating against a white policeman who shot an unarmed black hoodlum in Missouri. No one was surprised when non-whites burned police cars and buildings. It made no difference that witnesses verified the policeman's story, and witnesses disputed the non-white witness' story that the young man was killed while walking toward the police with his hands raised. Witnesses, all of the physical evidence and the autopsy verify the white policeman's story, yet rioters who aren't busy burning someone else's property continue to parade with their hands raised screaming, "Don't shoot!" If the young hoodlum who had robbed a store minutes earlier on video had done the same thing, he'd still be alive.

But he didn't. However, when non-white activists don't get the result they want, they claim it's not justice. Never mind what evidence says, white folks are unfair! Just watch network news for a few minutes on almost any day to view blatant racism. If the screaming, violent mobs this week didn't remind you of the Mau Mau uprising of the 1950s in Africa, you have forgotten some important lessons of history.

Oh, by the way, happy Halloween...

CHICKEN BUD

I'd been exposed to Bud McDonald at several annual meetings of the Texas Outdoor Writer Association where it was difficult to miss the larger than life outdoor writer. And the barrel-chested, funny man really came alive when alcohol found its way into his bloodstream. It found its way there frequently as friends pushed drinks at him to awaken his ready wit, not that he ever really needed any stimulation.

I got to know McDonald, the king of San Angelo outdoor writers, much better on a fateful trip several TOWA members made to Lake Guerrero, Mexico. When I arrived in Harlingen, Jim Foster, the writer who had organized the complimentary trip to a fine resort, picked me up at the airport and informed me that I would be driving the van into Mexico. It seems a horsie had stepped on Foster's foot forcing remedial surgery which scratched him from the travel list. Hence, since I was the first to arrive, I became the designated driver.

I was not overly excited about driving in Mexico, much less with an outdoor writer audience that I knew would be both critical and vocal. Worse yet, McDonald claimed the seat behind the driver. Oh, we got through the border crossing without too much trouble and a bribe of ten bucks, as I recall, protected us from a vehicle search. The problems began when we reached the narrow highways south of Matamoros. It seems it was the season to move those deep plows that were in heavy use at that time to convert brush country into tilled fields. Trucks carrying the massive machines bore no wide load warning signs; it was a definite oversight.

The lead van built quite a lead on us since it was piloted by a native driver. We didn't worry since we had a writer with us who knew the way and he spoke fluent Spanish in case we were stopped at any checkpoints. As I pulled a bit into the other lane to peek around one of the big trucks, I quickly jerked back into our lane to avoid an oncoming truck. McDonald roared in language I've cleaned up for the Sunday school audience, "Good grief, Gresham! What are you trying to do, get us all killed?"

After each aborted pass, McDonald asked something like, "Damn, Gresham, where did you learn to drive? Did you get your license from Sears?" The colorful insults lasted for a half hour or so – until McDonald discovered the unopened case of Scotch beneath his seat. He quickly cut the top off a beer can with his trusty Boy Scout knife and poured a liberal measure of Scotch into his makeshift highball glass.

The transformation wrought by a few ounces of amber liquid was astounding! The next time I nosed the van to the left and dodged back into my lane, McDonald loudly asked, "What's the matter, Gresham? Take a chance! No guts, no glory!" His conversations with the driver continued in that same vein until he began leading cheers. "Let's hear it for the driver! Hip, hip hooray! C'mon, let's hear it for Gresham!"

This was the final cock fight we saw on our writers' trip to Mexico. It had a dual distinction. It was the last fight I ever witnessed and the one that gave Bud McDonald his nickname.

We somehow survived the drive to enjoy a marvelous experience. After all, the lodge had invited Mexico's Minister of

Tourism to attend. We ate the finest T-bone steaks imaginable, had mariachi bands and – four cockfights. Yep, they still do that in Mexico. Well, McDonald fared badly in his bets on the first three birds and grumbled mightily about it. The lodge owner took him aside and told him how to judge the birds. "Don't pick the biggest cock," he advised. "Most of the time the smaller cocks are faster and they can slash the throats of the bigger, slower birds before they can get out of the way."

So, McDonald looked over the next pair during the preliminaries and shouted, "40 dollars on *rojo*!" although it was much smaller than the black cock.

"You're on," the owner said. McDonald's jaw dropped at the bet his mentor made against his own advice. Then he watched as the black cock cut *rojo* into chicken fingers, thus eliminating every last cent of McDonald's traveling money. From that day on, our late, great friend Bud McDonald was known as Chicken Bud by members of the Texas Outdoor Writers Association.

WHAT'S IN A NAME?

Deer hunting ain't what it used to be. Some things are better now, of course, but I miss the primitive pleasures of the 1960s and '70s. Few men hunt today like we did way back when. Most hunters today arrive at plush blinds on ATVs just before their corn feeders attract the bucks photographed by their game cams last week. Frankly, I miss the old days of sneaking through the woods, hoping to see my buck before he sees me.

Uncomfortable blinds caused a lot of our sneaking in the old days. But what the areas we hunted on the 1151-2/3-acre Kothmann Ranch lacked in comfort, they made up for with great names. Gordon Hubbard named one that comes to mind. Hubbard climbed a tall tree one day to sit in a fork at the top. When he got back to camp, he claimed the limb was so high he'd seen eagles circling beneath him. When we nailed steps up the tree and cross boards in the top fork the next day, we naturally christened it The Eagle's Nest.

We killed several deer from that tree, but you couldn't hunt it on a windy day. Well, you could, but no one could turn loose of a limb to take a shot. If you **were** brave enough to turn loose, you'd have to time your trigger squeeze to coincide with the instant your crosshairs swung past the deer again. It's tough to calculate reverse lead needed to compensate for limb sway.

Then there were the Twin Windmills, aptly named because that's exactly what it was, two windmills – with a rail corral sitting between side-by-side stock tanks (or ponds as non-Texans call them) fed by the two windmills. That old corral made a pretty fair blind and it provided a lot of activity during dry spells. A few hundred yards to the east stood The Old Man's Stand, a blind the rancher built for the days he chose to hunt with us. It had four walls and a roof, but none of them stopped much wind or water. And the old man considered it unmanly to sit down, so there was no built-in bench. Besides, all the openings were cut for standing shots.

Some names were simple, but everyone knew where they were. The Swale was a low spot that filled with water during spring rains and grew rye grass that attracted deer. Larry Pendleton spent a lot of time in the Swale. Then there was North of the Oat Patch, a big live oak favored by Clinton Metcalf. That's just as well, because the 6'-3" Metcalf installed the steps up to the 2X12 platform; he was one of the few who could reach the steps. Come to think of it, Metcalf also built West of the Oat Patch, a shorter tree, also with wide steps, overlooking trails through scattered bee brush.

We inherited some names from the rancher, specifically, the Horse Trap, the Bull Trap, the Y and the Turn-Around. My most vivid memory of the brushy Horse Trap was the doe Clinton shot while perched on a low tree limb. That old doe, big as a kudu bull, nearly herniated both of us as we tried to lift her over the fence. The Bull Trap was a big, brushy pasture that contained several blinds. The Mexican Shack, built by the rancher's hands, was heavily hunted. Like the old man's stand, it had a low, leaky roof and boards with wide cracks between them. The old man built blinds to conceal hunters, not to keep them warm and dry.

When Ft. Wolters gave away many large signs for buildings that had been phased out, Gordon Hubbard got a truck load of them for walls of new blinds. Thus, the Dry Cleaners bore its name on the side facing the county road. Chuck Eaton, when he wasn't in the Old Man's Stand, favored The Three Tree Stand, aptly named for the platform built between the trunks of three separate trees. It was a couple of hundred yards east of The Cultivator Seat. Yep, that one was a steel cultivator seat bolted to a horizontal live oak limb overlooking trails leading to the nearby 7-acre oat patch. It was a nice view, but the heads of huge lag bolts holding the seat in place got pretty hard after a few minutes.

We killed lots of deer Across the Creek – named because it was across the creek only about 100 yards from the cabin. That's where my dad shot his 12-point buck with double drop tines. It also marked the last blind my bride ever climbed into. Heck, it wasn't my fault that a raccoon had just pooped on the board where she put her hand in the dark. Besides, she killed an eight-point that morning despite the 'coon poop residue on her hands.

Clinton Metcalf, left, and the late Rinie Zimmerman survey the view from a new platform they built in the fencerow to the oat patch.

About 300 yards west of Across the Creek, the Creek Stand stood on the south bank of, you guessed it, the creek. Almost every hunter shot a deer from that stand in one year or another. And every hunter **did** shoot a deer from the Oat Patch. It wasn't really hunting, though; it was choosing. I remember counting 94 deer one evening in the field at the same time. Most of the time, we were too busy choosing a candidate for the table to count them.

My bride shot a buck there early one afternoon and she chose to stay in the blind while I field dressed her kill a few yards behind her blind. When I finished the job, I looked up and she waved me to stay down. I did and a few minutes later she shot another deer for me to field dress before I walked back for the truck.

We might have had some days there that weren't so great, but I prefer to remember the ones that were. There's a lifetime supply.

Back in November of 1976, Chuck Eaton shot this fine buck as it tried to sneak past the Old Man's Stand.

REPUTATIONS CAN BE DECEIVING

After being stung a few times by folks with sterling reputations, I adopted a, "Don't tell me what you can do; **show** me what you can do," attitude. It all began when I edited a fishing publication back in the early '80s. My publisher laid out his plans and told me he'd already hired a writer for the largemouth bass section. He was an old rodeo rider and a great bass fishing guide turned outdoor writer, and a good one, my publisher said. I selected the remaining writers and made the story assignments.

All the manuscripts submitted by my writers were excellent and required little editing, if any. My publisher's pick was a whole 'nother story. Well after it was due, the writer finally answered my call and agreed to deliver the finished copy… such as it was. The manuscript, handwritten on a Big Chief yellow tablet, was the first of several I would receive during my years as an editor. The writer handed it to me and said, "Ron said to write 2,000 words and cover black bass fishing during the four seasons. I reached 2,000 words before I got to winter tactics, so you can finish it."

Finish it, hell! I had to write the damned thing. I used his ideas when I could, but imagine what fun I had re-writing copy with such misspellings as "cain pol" and "minner bucket." I'll wager that it was the best thing Ron's "writer" ever got published. I questioned adding his byline to the finished piece after I had rewritten it and generated the fourth section myself, but the publisher insisted. He added a nice bonus for my extra work load, but it seemed like a lie to me.

A similar thing happened when I served as editor of *USA Outdoors Magazine* in 1985. The publisher allowed me to hire all writers and pick the stories – except for my Southeast Field Editor. My publisher had already hired a crackerjack writer, a Pulitzer Prize winner. We were lucky to get him, he said. Yeah, right. It started out like *deja vu* all over again, as Yogi said, and it stayed that way.

The first copy I got was typed, but the writing was atrocious. The first paragraph, for example, was seven lines long and the only punctuation was the period at the end. Yep, a seven-line sentence. Needless to say, I had to rewrite everything the fellow sent me, and he sent a lot! Sometimes I'd get five or six packets of odds and ends per week.

I soon instructed him to quit mailing bits and pieces of information and assemble them into one article per month in column form. He replied that he would send me everything he could think of and I could use the portions I liked. Well, I liked none of it, but this publisher was as stubborn as the other one. Instead of firing the prize winner, I was forced to re-write his material, making yet another writer look good. It turned out the guy had a Pulitzer Prize all right, but it was an award made to the newspaper he owned rather than an individual prize. I strongly suspect it was awarded for work done by someone other than the owner.

Old friend Leonard Ranne asked a lot of everyone he knew, but since no one worked harder than he did, we all tried to please him. Under his leadership, TBBU contributed over $500,000 to help build the Texas Freshwater Fisheries Center. Ranne was elected to the Texas Freshwater Fishing Hall of Fame in 2000.

A couple of years after leaving that magazine, I edited *Our Inland Fisheries* magazine for old friend Leonard Ranne. Like publishers before him, he suggested I use the work of this really good photographer/writer he knew. His manuscript, like the earlier editing debacle, was handwritten on yellow tablet paper! What is it with Big Chief tablets, anyway? This fellow had great ideas and wrote a few great phrases, but he couldn't coordinate them worth a damn. Nor did he use standard rules of spelling or grammar. To satisfy my old friend the publisher, though, I re-wrote several of his stories that year.

Several friends had encouraged me to enter the writing competitions of the Texas Outdoor Writers Association for several years, so I finally relented and entered three stories that year. Imagine my chagrin, if you will, when every one of my entries lost to stories I had rewritten for that fellow who couldn't write. When I was asked to enter later competitions, I told them I'd enter again after they started judging the original manuscripts instead of editors' corrections… or start giving the awards to the editors.

I have since won first place in several national and state competitions and second place money once, but don't talk to me about awards or reputations; I could care less about them. Just show me what you can do.

Leonard Ranne, then president of TBBU, accepted a $50,000 check from Johnny Morris and Bass Pro Shops, the first major contribution toward the Texas Freshwater Fisheries Center in Athens.

SHOOTIN' AT THE LAW

I've always enjoyed having a lawman on a deer lease or in a boat with me, not because it provides any advantage when dealing with other law enforcement personnel. No matter what protesters say, if you don't do anything wrong, you don't need an advantage. But before right to carry permits, it was nice to have someone around who was legally armed at all times and knew what to do if trouble came lookin' for us.

Dallas Police Officer Clinton L. Metcalf was our resident protector and legal eagle on the Kothmann Ranch lease near Castell, Texas. In addition to being a great pistol shot, he was a good fisherman, a successful hunter, a pretty darned good domino player and a good story teller around the old wood stove. C.L. was also dependable and punctual – until that Sunday morning in the mid-'70s when he was late getting back to camp for our trek home to Oak Cliff.

Just as I decided to go look for him, C.L. stormed into the cabin in obvious distress, shaking and muttering to himself. When we asked what was wrong, he answered, "The SOBs tried to shoot me!" Now that's a scary statement right there to hear from a policeman. As he calmed a bit, the story unfolded.

As C.L. sneaked through the bull trap pasture looking for a doe, he saw movement that prompted him to kneel for a look through his scope. As he weighed his options, the background behind the deer suddenly revealed a scoped rifle aimed at him! He flattened against the ground just a rifle bullet clipped through the leaves just above his head. C.L. jumped up and shouted at the man who had fired at a deer that stood directly between them. The poacher kneeling in the county road that ran through our ranch had illegally fired at the deer, narrowly missing C.L.

At his shout, the camo-clad poacher scrambled back into a pickup truck, C.L hadn't seen and drove deeper into our ranch. The strangers didn't realize that an aluminum gate blocked the county road on our western boundary. C.L. figured they might turn around and come out the way they had come in, so he hurried over to the road, climbing over the fence just as he heard the truck returning. He stood in the center of the road waving them to halt, but they didn't plan to stop. When the truck veered into the bar ditch to go around him, C.L. fired a round through the truck bed, chambered a second round and had just found the driver in his scope when a moment of better judgment saved the illegal hunter's life. The noise from the business end of a 7 mm magnum is horrendous at close range! The truck stopped and two frightened young men emerged with their hands in the air. My enraged friend, at 6'-3" and 215 pounds, and wielding a rifle he'd just shown them he wasn't afraid to use, was a scary sight.

C.L. gave them the tongue-lashing of their lives, reminding them they could easily have killed him and driven away without even knowing he was there. He got their Texas drivers licenses, made them write down all their information and checked the information for accuracy. He chewed on them a little more, he said, then sent them on their way.

"Clinton! Why didn't you hold them for the Sheriff or the Game Warden?" I asked.

"I just wanted them out of my sight. I was so mad that I was afraid I'd kill them," he explained.

Instead, C.L. passed along all the information on the two hunters to Louis Kothmann, the landowner, and provided statements to all interested agencies. So, the hunters were probably lucky they only had to answer to Llano County lawmen and State Game Wardens. Oh, the State ran them down and they paid big fines and lost their hunting rights, but they were in one piece. I forget the actual figures, but I remember thinking at the time that their fines amounted to megabucks in that era.

C.L. Metcalf remained a legendary figure in the Hill Country for a while after that. The Sheriff knew him as did Texas Parks & Wildlife Department personnel. And anyone who'd ever met Louis Kothmann heard about it. The old rancher got lots of talking mileage out of that experience. Warden Swope visited our camp just to talk with Clinton, and after Swope retired, the younger wardens always stopped by for coffee and conversation the night before season openings. I don't know it for a fact, but I'll bet the lawmen even kept an eye on our lease when we weren't there.

I believe in making friends of our peacekeepers – and trust me, accidental or not, you really don't ever want to shoot at the law…

When he wasn't apprehending poachers or hunting deer, Clinton Metcalf was a fair-to-middlin' dove shooter.

In addition to being a good hunter, Clinton Metcalf was a handy fella around a camp house. He was the undisputed master at coaxing flames into the old wood stove.

THE WORLD WAS OUR PLAYGROUND

Thank God I grew up during the 1940s and '50s! That was an era of innocence compared to the frightening conditions of today. Our parents ordered us out of the house to play; folks today are afraid to let children out of their sight. Of course, our leashes might have been shortened somewhat if our parents knew about some of our close calls – or maybe not. They grew up much as we did, in God's great outdoors, the finest playground ever conceived.

We enjoyed a few more manmade toys than our parents had, but, generally, we played with whatever we could find. And we learned valuable lessons from our interaction with nature, even if it was only identifying which tree bark was most likely to scrape our bare skin. Hackberries were the worst; piss ellums were rough; live oaks were better, but rougher than red oaks. Chinaberry trees were the smoothest, but the brittle branches caused worse problems than scraped skin. I learned the hard way that even lightweights can't crawl very far onto Chinaberry limbs without risking a broken limb, maybe one of your own. Luckily, I landed on my head and didn't need a cast…

Kids today hurt themselves on expensive trampolines; we used grapevines, free for the climbing. When we sharecropped the Bustle farm near Patillo, grapevines covered large sections of the creek that ran through the west pasture. One year when Daddy took a ladder out to a large tree to pick the mustang grapes that covered it, I discovered that the vines were strong enough to support the body weight of a 12-year-old boy. A few days later that knowledge led to a successful assault on the summit of Mount Grapevine.

Getting to the top was just the beginning. After carefully probing the canopy, a safety check of sorts, we found that running, jumping and rolling provided much the same sensation as jumping on a bed – without maternal interference. We were careful around the edges because it was a long way to the ground, but we failed to make any scientific tests to determine the effects of wear and tear on the green canopy. On second thought, I suppose I WAS the test. Test results clearly showed that when leaves and smaller vines are compromised by heavy use, it will no longer support the weight of a boy of any age. I plummeted feet first through the canopy, but luckily my fall was stopped some 15 feet above the dry creek bed below. Unfortunately, straddling the large vine that ended my fall temporarily turned me into a tenor. Fortunately, the new voice pitch WAS temporary, but the fall took all the fun out of vine running, I can tell you.

So, it was back to the old red tile barn with the B-B gun. On a good day, I'd get a shot at one of the huge barn rats (Dad called 'em wharf rats) that grew quite fat on the oats and maize we stored there. In the absence of any other game, there was always the red wasp nest in the southeast corner of the barn.

Things we remember from our youth always loom larger than life in our memory banks, but I **know** that nest was as large as the diameter of a basketball. It just kept getting larger, year by year, even as I trimmed chunks off the nest by grouping shots closely enough together to slice through the nest, widening the cut until a piece fell off. I worked pretty hard at the task, but those persistent wasps just kept gaining ground. The last time I drove down 281 in Erath County, all of the structures I remembered on the Bustle farm were gone. I'll bet the weight of a huge wasp nest finally caused the roof collapse and ultimate destruction of our old red barn.

Hey, it could happen!

I'VE EARNED THE RIGHT

On one of my several trips to Mexico with the Texas Outdoor Writers Association (TOWA), I was delighted to see Sig Badt walk up to the Southwest Airlines counter. For a fellow in his 80s, Sig was unbelievably active. He was full of it ... and vinegar, too. I waved as he turned to find a seat and watched him make his way toward me.

"Hello, Gresham!" said the smiling Badt. "Are you flying down for this outdoor writer thing?"

"Yes, I am," I answered. "I'm glad you are, too."

"Yes," he said. "Listen, did you drive to the airport in your truck?"

"Yes, I did."

"Are you flying back Sunday afternoon?" he continued.

I gave him another affirmative answer.

"Oh, good," he sighed, "I might need to catch a ride home with you."

"Sure," I agreed. "Are you having car trouble?"

"No," Badt replied. "It's the wife. She's mad at me and she might not come back here to pick me up."

"What did you do to make her mad, Sig?" I inquired.

"I just told her I was coming on this fishing trip and she got mad! She says to me, 'You old fool, you've had two heart attacks, open-heart heart surgery, you've had two cancers and you're 83 years old! And that Lake Guerrero is like an ocean! What if you die out in the middle of that ocean?' 'What better place?' I asked. That's why I may need a ride."

Well, old Sig is gone now, but he didn't fulfil his wife's fears that trip. In fact, I made another TOWA trip to the same lake with him a couple of years later. He lived through that one, too.

The late Sig Badt was one of those old curmudgeons who didn't mind telling you what he thought. If you didn't want to know his opinion, you'd better not ask him. That's why he hung around with a bunch of young writer types. We always asked the questions we knew would stir him up; we loved his answers. An angry Sig Badt was a man you could learn from.

There was always something to stir him up in Mexico; a country full of backward folks will do that to an old timer once in a while. When he got back to the lodge once after his first day on the water, someone asked him how his fishing had been. "Terrible!" he grumbled. "This kid we had for a guide went through the trees like it was a race track. When we'd tell him to slow down, he'd go faster. We bounced off trees like a pin ball machine. My guide can't even laugh in English!"

On the final morning of that trip, Sig speared a slice of honeydew melon, took a big bite before announcing, 'This is the worst melon I've ever tasted. It's green!"

One of our group suggested we should be more grateful to our hosts who had given us free transportation, rooms, boats and guides and, generally, great food. "That doesn't give them a right to serve melon that tastes like this!" Sig insisted.

Once when someone gently chastised Sig for being grouchy, he responded with a line I've copied on occasion. "I'm 83 years old," he said, "I've earned the right!"

DEATH VALLEY, TEXAS

Our group of hunters followed the same tradition anytime we moved to a new hunting lease. We drew numbers from a hat with the hunter drawing number one picking first and on down the line to the poor guy stuck with number 12. When we leased the Winters Ranch four miles north of Evant in 1989, Mike Moore, of the Pat and Mike twins combo, drew a low number, first pick, I think. Whatever, he chose the canyon he wanted and told us about it at every opportunity.

The hunters who leased the ranch before we did told Mike they called the canyon Death Valley because so many deer died there. It was a fine looking horseshoe canyon, probably 300 yards across the mouth from rim to rim. The floor had scattered openings, but the steep, brushy canyon walls were difficult for humans to walk through; deer had no problems navigating the thicket. And deer died in Death Valley, to be sure, but not nearly as many as Mike saw. From his tower on the north rim, he could see deer moving over a goodly portion of the county, 99% of them out of range. It was a lo-o-o-ong shot from his tower to his feeder on the floor below, but he and his brother connected on a few shots.

My favorite Death Valley stories didn't involve whitetail deer. One narrative involved Mike's treasured Indiana Jones hat. As he told it, he was negotiating his way down the rocky trail at the mouth of the canyon after dark one day when a rattlesnake sounded off from a distance not nearly far enough away to suit him. Now, I suppose Mike was as coordinated as the rest of us, but he will never be a contestant on *Dancing with the Stars*. Trust me on that; it will make the mental picture I'll try to paint a little more vivid. Mike was not a little fellow, so when he described his stumbling, half-falling effort to put distance between him and the snake, we could see the dance clearly. Then he plaintively related, "And I lost my Indiana Jones hat!"

It was a jolly night in camp as we laughed over and over about Mike losing his hat to a rattlesnake. He chose not to search for his lost hat in the dark. He left the trail and the hat, to the snake. Unfortunately, the hat endured a rain that night before Mike found it the next morning. I'm not sure whether he ever nursed it back to health or not. He'd rather not discuss hats or snakes.

On another day, yet another Death Valley critter topped the camp discussion. Mike came back to camp telling about a funny looking deer he'd seen in the bottom of the canyon. It was big, he said, but the funny thing was, it had a long, heavy tail, a tail as long as its body. His twin Pat immediately started on him, as only a twin brother can do, berating him for not recognizing a mountain lion when he saw one. It's not unusual for a hunter to fail to recognize a common animal when he has another species on his mind, but Pat kept up the pressure. The ranch manager had told Pat about a big lion being spotted several times in the area and we later found its huge tracks along the moist creek bottom. It was lucky for the lion that the other twin hadn't been there that day... maybe.

The one deer I remember from Death Valley fell to my old buddy Larry Pendleton on Thanksgiving Day. He decided he wanted to rattle up a buck on that foggy morning, so we walked up to Death Valley from the south and dropped into it just below the south rim. As I rattled and blew on my new grunt call a few yards from Larry, we began to hear grunts below us. After long minutes, we watched the buck carefully sneak toward us as I tried to sound exactly like another buck and nothing else.

Then, when my buddy finally got a clear shot and dropped the eight point buck, we celebrated with high fives and back slaps until we had finished field dressing his deer. Then we discovered our only option for getting him back to camp was a climb **UP** the steep wall; it was far too thick and too far to ever get through the thicket with him. I sounded like a twin brother as I reminded him over and over to shoot deer on the tops of hills, not down steep walls. Shoot up, drag down, I told him, not vice versa.

Sigh-h-h-h, I loved Death Valley...

ENGAGE BRAIN, OPEN MOUTH

One old saying, overused but still so true, goes something like this: A person may keep his mouth shut and appear dumb, or he can open his mouth and remove all doubt. I'd like to think I've always avoided appearing dumb, but no one wins them all so I don't worry about it. I do, however, try to restrict my opinions to subjects of which I have a fair degree of understanding. Surprise, surprise, I just happened to meet a couple of women a few weeks ago who should have adhered to the old, overused saying. Oh, yeah, they really did, no doubt at all – and, bigger surprise, I endured it with nary a whimper... a mild objection, but no whimper.

It all began innocently enough, at the end of a nice day. We had boarded the free bus to the Choctaw Casino in Durant, Oklahoma, that morning and spent the afternoon trying to make it up to those Indians for relieving them of almost all their land. It didn't work; we brought home some of their money to go along with whatever loot our ancestors passed down to us. So, it was a happy bus ride home down US 75. As we rolled down the highway just south of Howe, I saw a huge cloud of dust rolling across the horizon and crossing all lanes of the highway.

"I wonder what that dust is, Gene?" I said to our driver from our seat right behind him.

"I don't know," he answered.

As we got nearer, I exclaimed, "Oh, that's a corn harvester running through the cornfield! Boy, it's throwing up a lot of dust!"

At that point, Ms. Inez commented from her seat across the aisle, "That's not corn, they're bailin' maize. Any fool knows they don't bail corn!"

What I thought to myself was, *Duh, that's right because that big old self-propelled machine ain't a hay bailer*, but what I said was, "No, that's corn."

Having been raised on a farm working in corn fields, maize patches, peanut patches and cotton fields and hating anything to do with bailing Johnson grass hay, I felt I was on pretty solid ground. And then, boys and girls, I was reminded of a chauvinistic proverb: You can tell a woman, but you can't tell her much.

Ms. Davis, sitting right across the aisle from us, in the seat in front of Ms. Inez, added, "That sho' nuff ain't corn. Inez is right. They was big bales of hay laying in front of that maize right along this road last week. They jus' bailin' the rest of it."

"No, ma'am," I said, "it's a corn harvester cutting off the stalks and stripping the kernels off the ears of corn near the bottom of the stalks. The dust is from the stalks and cobs being chewed up."

Then, for the second time in approximately 30 seconds, Ms. Inez called me a fool. Well, she didn't phrase it exactly that way. She just repeated, "That's not corn, they're bailin' maize. Any fool knows they don't bail corn!"

I opened my mouth again, but before I could utter another word, my bride elbowed my ribs and whispered, "You might as well be quiet. You can't win."

Well, sir, that was probably the hardest thing I ever did, not counting explaining to my Daddy why I was getting so green around the gills. You see, I knew more about corn and maize than I knew about Brown Mule chewing tobacco. And this little white farm boy knew more by age ten than those two women – about corn and maize, that is. I won't make a blanket statement despite my suspicions.

So, I sat there chewing my tongue, trying to smile as the two women ganged up on the fool. "See that maize field over there? Any fool knows that's not corn!" one would say. The other would agree and then repeat the process at the next field. I didn't tell them that anyone could see the kernels flowing out of the chute into the corn truck rolling alongside the corn harvester. Nor did I tell them that hay bailers don't run through fields cutting and bailing hay at 20 miles per hour. Hay fields are mowed first, then hay rakes sweep it into narrow rows for a bailer to roll slowly above the row, picking it up and rolling it into bales. Nor did I tell them that those things that could be seen clearly on top of the stalks were corn tassels and the three or four little pointy things hanging off each stalk were ears of corn. Nope, I didn't say any of that.

My bride was right; the longer they talked, the dumber they sounded. I later heard from other riders that anybody who knew what a cornstalk looked like knew who the dumb ones were. No one wanted to stand up, though, to a couple of loud and argumentative women maybe mean enough to whip us.

Please note how mellow I've become in my old age. I haven't once used the word "stupid," although a wise man once said, "Stupid is as stupid does."

Undoubtedly, two ill-informed women still think they're right and that they won an argument. They weren't, and they didn't. In fact, they didn't engage one brain cell before opening those mouths. Pity, they could have learned something about farming. I hope they do before someone else finds out which ones are fools.

CHILDLESS WITH KIDS

Pay close attention now; otherwise you'll never understand how a married couple with no children, natural or adopted, could possibly end up with a daughter, three grandchildren and a passel of great-grandchildren. First, my bride and I love children, but none of them turned out to be ours. We got no closer than a single miscarriage …. and suddenly we were way past childbearing age.

It was all Floyd Rogers' fault; my co-worker encouraged me to try the Mexican food at Amaya's, a little place on the square in Lancaster. So, innocently enough, Bettie and I drove with neighbors Joyce and Louie Duncan to the little restaurant. After we'd finished a tasty meal served by a vivacious little waitress, owner Pablo Esparza asked me what we thought of Nancy, our waitress. "She's so cute," I said, "that I'm thinking of adopting her."

Well, she was.

The experience was so good that we made another trip to Amaya's the next Saturday night. As we walked into the restaurant, a cute little Mexican maiden ran toward us yelling, "Daddy! Daddy! Daddy!"

"W-w-wh-h-h-a-a-at!" I stuttered.

"Pablo told me you were going to adopt me!" she told me.

So it began… Venancia Nava called me Daddy forever after and everyone at Amaya's called her my daughter. After a couple of months she brought her husband Javier and their children to introduce them to Gramma and Grampa. And, as easily as that, they became our grandchildren Jesse, Junior and Marissa. When we had a block party, our neighbors and all their families came for food, drink and music. Our new family attended as well and the relationship blossomed.

We followed them through years of grade school, high school, girlfriends, lost girlfriends, loss of birth parents, a quinceanera and a wedding. We didn't see enough of them when Nancy left Amaya's to go to college. But after her graduation and that great party to celebrate her Associate Degree, she tired of her new job with the college and returned to her first love. She became the manager of the second Amaya's, this one in Red Oak, even closer to our home in Ovilla.

Jesse, Nancy and Junior, September, 1996

The grandkids are all grown now and Jesse and Marissa have kids of their own. Jesse and Junior operate a store with their father called, appropriately, Nava's Tires in Red Oak. The Navas bought some rural acreage and Junior discovered a new passion; he became a bonafide cattle rancher. Through the years, Nancy's kids worked at Amaya's as our waiters, as did the other relatives.

We also became good friends at Amaya's with Nancy's brother-in-law and sister-in-law, Erasmo and Estella Nava, as well as their son Allen and daughter Elizabeth. Estella's nieces, the three Muñoz sisters Angie, Claudia and Michelle, took their turns working at Amaya's; the baby girl Michelle is already in college, but still works a few shifts there.

Our friendships with Estella's sisters and nieces have made our assumed family as large as our birth families, thereby insuring quinceaneras, graduation celebrations and weddings for a long time. Allen is in college in Paris and it's less than two years until Elizabeth's quinceanera. Cecilia Najera and Brenda Quiroz are two more lovely Estella nieces in our adopted family.

Amaya's also hosted my bride's surprise 70th birthday party. That was nice because my niece Ashlea and her husband Levi got to meet their cousins Nancy and Marissa they never knew about. Maybe we'll think about requesting Amaya's as the location for our memorial celebrations….

But I digress. On August 30, 2010, Marissa posted a message for me on Facebook. "Hey, Grampa, I stole ur book from mom and ima have to try some of ur recipes. I been looking for a guide and where better to look. Have a great day."

The greatest thing about that post was the post from my nephew Sean Pruett, BS's oldest son. He wrote, "Uncle Morris, I know, I've been gone for a long time and haven't been around the family much, but I didn't know you had any kids. How did you get a granddaughter?"

So, now you also know how a childless old couple found themselves part of a wonderful second family.

Joyce Duncan, Nancy, Marissa and Javier Nava, September, 1996

My bride enjoyed her 70th birthday party with family and friends at Amaya's

COMPETITIVE GARDENING

I had never looked at gardening as fun; it was something I did to put tasty veggies at my fingertips. They do taste better out of your own garden; it's not a myth. But fun never figured into the equation. Then 7-year-old Christopher Hale wandered into my garden from across the street and turned it into a fun thing. Chris, his sister Danielle and his mother Carolyn lived with his grandparents at the time he became interested in all the tall plants in my garden. I gave Chris the grand tour, explaining each vegetable and what each type looked like when it was ready to be picked.

He immediately asked me if he could help me pick the garden every day after he got home from school. Of course, I said yes, but we had "the talk." It was understood that it was my garden and I was the boss. He could help me as long as he did what I told him. He minded well and he asked plenty of questions about how to do things.

It didn't take long for the chore to become competitive. For Chris, it became a multi-colored Easter egg hunt. He wanted to find the biggest tomato and the largest pepper, pick the most squash and find the longest cucumber. And who wouldn't deliberately overlook a humongous cantaloupe so a kid can find it? Good rains and moderate temperatures led to bumper crops of everything that summer, so it was no problem for Chris to find plenty of tomatoes, peppers, cucumbers, squash and cantaloupes.

The problem was locating enough folks to take the excess. For example, the cantaloupe harvest lasted three weeks gave us 20 to 25 big melons EVERY DAY. Christopher brought his Little Tykes wagon over every day to carry them to the house; it took two trips every day. I'd carry a couple of five-gallon buckets of stuff to work every day and I'd leave enough melons at the DeSoto Gun Club for almost every shooter in the league to take one. I was never so glad to see the end of a crop in my life!

The most important thing about the garden that year, though, was that it showed me how hard it is to rear a child properly. One night when we were coming out of a restaurant, Christopher acted just like a boy his age. He started shinnying up the crape myrtle tree beside the front door. I told him to get down, that the owner wouldn't want little boys to get hurt on his tree. He kept climbing and I told him in a little louder voice to cease and desist. Well, the little dickens kept going until his brook-no-nonsense grandfather came outside. Louie ended the game without delay.

Christopher Hale displays his one-day harvest of cantaloupes
July 1996

My lesson came the next afternoon when Chris came home from school to find me in the garden. He quickly put on his rubber galoshes, grabbed his pail and came running over. "You started without me!" he accused.

"That's because you don't get to pick today," I said.

"Why can't I?" he asked.

"Do you remember the little talk we had and I told you that you could help me pick only if you minded me?" I asked.

"Uh-huh," he admitted.

"Well, you didn't mind me when I told you to quit climbing that tree. I can't have a helper who won't do what I say. Do you understand that?"

"I can't pick any more?" he wailed.

"Not today," I answered. "Go home and think about it and we'll see about tomorrow."

Folks, let me tell you, I almost relented as I watched my little buddy trudge home, shoulders and head bowed, with his little bucket no longer swinging. But I didn't call him back.

Thank goodness he was a quick learner; he never again disobeyed me. I had a great helper until school friends and girls began intruding on his thoughts. Then, after his grandfather was killed, Chris planted his own garden where his "Poppa" once had one. Well, Chris is a full-grown workin' man now and owner of his own house. I'm not sure whether he has anything planted now or not, but I'll wager he will never forget how it's done. Once a kid gets dirt under his fingernails, the farming virus gets into his bloodstream.

Really...

Blonde bombers Christopher and Danielle Hale, March 1996

CRITTERS ARE FUN TO WATCH

If a person hangs out in the woods very much, he soon learns that humans are not the only mammals that have adorable babies. Spotted whitetail fawns are cute, of course, without even trying. Maybe it's the spots, because the bobcat triplets I watched one morning were covered with them. Those short-tailed kitties, as mischievous as their domesticated cousins, jumped, rolled, waged mock fights and inspected everything that moved. If I'd had a ball of twine, I think I could have lured one into my lap. On second thought, maybe one's lap is not the place for those sharp little claws. Never mind…

I still laugh when I think of the antics of a spindly-legged fawn I saw one early November morning. Dozens of bright spots indicated that it must have been a really late fawn; its antics did nothing to dispute that opinion. As its mother grazed up a little draw, I watched the fawn sprint from one point to another before relocating his mother and running back to check the dinner table. Tired of the foolishness, she'd whack him with a hind leg and off he'd go again.

As the doe grazed within forty yards of my seat against the trunk of a live oak tree, her offspring raced willy nilly through the little glade. Finally, he sprinted directly toward me and showed off a 4-legged, sliding stop that ended a couple of feet from my outstretched boots (plenty close enough to establish his gender). Then he raised his head and stared intently at the funny looking stump. He flared and cupped his ears, then dropped his head, jerking it up just a couple of seconds later to trick the unknown lump into movement.

He turned his head to check on mom before raising and lowering his head over and over, examining me from every angle. My decision to check his reflexes with a quick flip of my hand generated a show suitable for *Funniest Home Videos*. Four spindly legs shot off in all directions as the little dickens almost fell on his chin. After he got his legs under him, he streaked toward his mama, sliding to a stop beneath her stomach, and stretched his neck around her hind leg for another look at what scared him.

Like a mother of any species would have done, the doe looked down at her little pest, then brushed him aside with another step. The little fella looked toward me again, then back at mama. After several looks, he forgot his earlier terror and returned to his "let's see if this will hack mama off" antics. He was still jumping and running as they slowly moved out of sight.

On another afternoon as I sat with bride in a blind overlooking an oat patch, deer began to funnel into the field about 75 yards away. She slowly slid her rifle out the window and discovered other deer back inside the woods. She watched intently through her rifle scope for a buck to suit her. Suddenly a couple of fawns ran into the field and began playing only 15 yards or so in front of us.

I whispered to Bettie to move slowly and try not to spook them. She whispered back that she'd seen them, but she also saw a buck she'd like to shoot if it came into the open. One of the little rascals ran toward us and stopped close enough to spit on. I touched Bettie's arm to warn her and hoped the fawn would move on into the field without spooking the herd. The fawn looked comical as he contentedly chewed oat stems that stuck out both sides of his mouth – until Bettie's rifle roared. Then, his legs flew in all directions.

The sound must have been deafening at his location just five feet from the muzzle. Either the noise or the concussion caused the fawn to fall on his butt in his haste to escape. After a quick glance verified Bettie's buck was down, I watched the fawn's wobbling getaway into the safety of the trees. Bettie missed the show; she'd filled her buck tags instead.

The outdoor experience offers an endless supply of entertainment. I'll never forget the three crows that flew down to surround a much smaller chaparral. As they tried to bully the bird that did not resemble the roadrunner of cartoon fame at all, he stood his ground. When the largest crow strutted up and leaped into the air, the speedy little bird responded with a classic chest bump, prompting the bullies to walk away. It was the same thing human bullies often do when they meet resistance.

One October when we still had quail in Stephens County, I sat in a bow blind near a corn feeder and watched three different coveys of bobwhites drop by for free meals. Everything would have been fine except that one of the coveys circled back for seconds before the third covey had finished. THAT was a show! Bobs might be small, but they're tough; there were chest bumps and clawing just as entertaining as game cock battles in Mexico.

Yep, critters are fun to watch, better than TV every time...

Whitetail deer such as this yearling doe are always entertaining. It's more fun, though, if they have curious young'uns with them.

SOMETIMES THE PLAN FAILS

One of the events at the good ol' Mineral Wells High School of yesteryear was the special assembly near the end of the school year. I probably wouldn't even remember the darned thing if not for my participation in the segment where upper classmen willed possessions to underclassmen.

First, a little background: Mrs. Fiedler was famous for her self-designed syllabus. Every student in her class received a copy of her mimeographed syllabus and was expected to answer the questions inside and be prepared to discuss those answers in class. We rarely opened the textbook because it took at least five different history reference books to find the answers.

Mrs. Fiedler had several inviolate rules, the most important of which was: You turned in your syllabus at the end of the year or you didn't get a passing grade. She refused to chance a student finding an old copy and profiting by the research of others.

So, I thought it might raise an eyebrow or two if I willed my completed Syllabus to an underclassman who shall remain unnamed. He knows who he is! It went off like clockwork – until I tried to find the young man after the Friday assembly. I looked everywhere for him throughout the lunch period. He had disappeared! He didn't return to classes that afternoon and he refused to answer phone calls at home that night or the next day. I drove hundreds of miles that weekend, expensive despite the low cost of gasoline (probably 17.9-cents per gallon).

I was frantic; the Syllabus was due on Monday! If I didn't turn it in, I got no grade in American History. Besides wreaking havoc on my grade average, I couldn't graduate without that course! All I knew for sure of was that young whippersnapper was a walking dead man if I didn't get that Syllabus before class time.

I'd figured out pretty early what he was doing. We didn't have scanners and copiers then; everything was copied in laborious handwriting. So, my choice of heirs was in hiding with lots of paper; and he was writing like he'd never written before. I'm sure the statute of limitations has run out on penalizing him for the theft of data for illicit purposes. I hardly think the use of his identity is enough punishment for my near cardiac arrest, so I'll just keep it between me and anyone who asks instead of giving him any free publicity.

    I got the Syllabus back, turned it in and got my grade. I doubt that Mrs. Fiedler ever compared my Syllabus to the one turned in by the unidentified copier of my work, despite her use of my Syllabus as her class copy for several years after that. Nor did she notice him using my exact words in any of his class discussions. How do I know? The boy graduated, that's how…

NO DAMNED DOGS IN THE HOUSE

I'd been looking at birddogs in the newspaper classifieds every morning for weeks, so it should have come as no surprise to my bride when I said, "I need the checkbook today."

"What for?" she asked.

"I'm driving to Garland to look at a Brittany spaniel after work today," I answered. "If they're as good as they sound, I'm going to buy one."

"We're not going to buy a damned dog!" she challenged.

She changed her tune when I walked into the house that afternoon and gave her checkbook back.

"Well, did you buy one?" she asked.

"Yes, I did. I think he's really going to be a good one – and he's beautiful," I told her.

Now, here's the change of tune: "We're not going to have a damned dog in the house," she insisted.

"Well, he's only four weeks old," I told, "and I can't pick him up until he's seven weeks old. That gives me three weeks to get a place fixed for him in the garage."

Therefore, when I brought Brandy home that frigid Wednesday evening, I bypassed the house and took him through the side gate and straight to the unattached garage. I introduced him to a new doghouse equipped with a heating light with stainless steel food and water dishes beside it. The little pot-bellied wonder tore into the puppy chow, but not for long. He was more interested in playing, probably a little lonesome without his mama and seven littermates.

"I thought you were bringing that dog home today," Bettie said when I walked into the house for supper.

"I did. He's eating his supper and looking over his new doghouse," I replied, and I was rewarded with only an answering grunt.

I spent most of my time at home down at the garage for the next couple of days, including a 30-minute visit every morning before leaving for work. The word "dog" was not mentioned during that time. Maybe she thought I was mowing the lawn.

Then, I brought Brandy out into the huge backyard on Saturday morning to play and see how he would react to a quail wing tied to a fly line. At seven weeks, he already would point the wing, often for as long as ten seconds, before trying to grab it. Then I'd put the wing away and play some more to keep him from tiring of not catching the wing.

Bettie stood outside much of that time, just watching the clumsy pup fall over his own feet at times, giggling at his antics. When I called him and started toward the garage, she asked, "Where are you going?"

"To put him back in the garage," I replied.

"Why don't you bring him in the house for a while?"

"Because you told me we weren't going to have a damned dog in the house," I reminded her.

"It won't hurt to bring him in for a little while," she conceded, "but there aren't going to be any dogs on the furniture."

And that, boys and girls, is how you train a wife into accepting a bird dog. You're already thinking ahead, aren't you? I can hear the gears turning. Well, you're right. When I asked her how he got up on our king size bed, she simply said, "I lifted him up here. He'll be all right – but we're not going to have a dog sleeping with us." Please note the retraction of demands and the use of the word "dog" without the "damned" modifier.

He was so perfect that I never had to teach him anything. He did what he was supposed to do before I could tell him. He pointed his first covey at ten weeks of age. I had just flushed a single quail and thought Brandy smelled where it had been. When he refused to budge at my call, I moved to pull him away and a covey of 20 birds flushed wildly. Without hesitating, Brandy jumped after the birds, but stopped at my "whoa" after a ten foot run.

At four months, he ran around and past a running covey and nudged them back toward me without flushing them. At a year old, he pointed a bird with a retrieved bird in his mouth. And he did all that for 13-1/2 years before my bride made me retire him because she thought the grand old dog would have a heart attack.

Of course, Brandy wasn't a "damned" dog, and I might never have had one if Bettie hadn't suggested that I find a female Brittany to keep Brandy from being lonesome when we were gone. I did, but I should have known what happens when you bring a strange female home – especially if she's a bitch….

Joe Gresham approaches a covey pointed by Gresham's Little Brandy, the finest bird dog I ever killed a quail over.

JOKES IN THEIR GENES

I didn't know what I was getting into when I married a Nevil; Bettie's father and mother were long divorced and I'd never met her father. Bettie's little brother was only 16 so there were no real indicators yet. A couple of years later, I met the late Jim Nevil, then I watched Bettie's brother become more like him every year.

Damn!

When we made our first visit to the Nevil hacienda near Crosby, I quickly noted that Jim was a lot like his uncle, the late Martin Cole; they were both full of it. You've heard of shade-tree mechanics; Martin, Jim – and now Ray – were/are shade-tree comedians. They didn't do it for money, but you laughed anyway.

Jim always had a pig or three, a couple of horses, a few cows in the pasture, usually a couple of donkeys and a red rooster followed by a flock of laying hens. Like a lot of the old line farmers, Jim went to bed early and got up well before daylight. On our first visit, and every one after that, he'd call to his sleepy daughter about 4:30 or so and if she didn't get up immediately, he'd come in and squeeze her big toe until she got out of bed, questioning his ancestry with every step.

My bride helps her father, Jim Nevil, prepare a vaccination needle.

When it got just light enough to see, Jim took Bettie and Ray out to the barn to help feed the stock. After spreading some hay, Jim told Bettie to get him a bucket of feed out of a wooden barrel in the corner.

"Where's the feed bucket?" she asked.

"Hanging on that nail over there," he answered.

So, she got the bucket, lifted the lid and the angry possum inside bared its teeth and hissed at her. She ran backward, screamed, "You SOB!" and threw the bucket at Jim. Both he and Ray were bent over with laughter. It became obvious after a while that he saved practical jokes just for his daughter.

His son Ray Nevil saves nothing, though. He is an equal opportunity trickster. He picks on everybody. His daughters Kim and Kelly endured it until they were grown and gone; now they try to ignore him. His grandkids, though, represent a brand new set of victims.

Kim's daughter Taylor Newlin, Ray's granddaughter, was in her third year of college at UT-San Antonio on a combination of golf and scholastic scholarships when several of us met one day for lunch. We knew Taylor had a feller and we suspected that it was more than a fleeting thing when she flew to Canada to meet his parents the previous Christmas.

So, before anyone had taken a bite of salad, Ray started the inquisition. At 21, Taylor already knew the drill, but she wasn't looking forward to it.

"This boy's folks, do they live where there are airports so I can fly up there – or do I have to drive," Ray asked.

'They live near an airport," Taylor answered, "Why do you want to know?"

"Because I'm going up there to see them so I'll know what kind of people they are," he revealed.

"You're going up to see them!" she squealed.

"Somebody's got to," he said. "What do they eat?"

"What do you mean, what do they eat?" Taylor asked.

"I mean do they eat the same food we do?" he explained.

"Yes!" Taylor declared in exasperation. "They live in Canada! They eat the same things we like!"

"Okay," he replied. "What do they do for a living?"

"They're both anesthesiologists," Kim answered.

"I don't care where they go to church!" Ray growled. "What do they do for a living?"

Both Kim's and Taylor's heads hit the table simultaneously. Her feller must be a good one; he's been warned about Ray and is still around a couple of years later. At least Louis got the warning I never received...

Look closely at the eyes. If the glint in Ray Nevil's eyes survives the rigors of printing, that's the devil you're looking at right there. That's what that is; I don't care what anybody says...

BEYOND YOUR FRONT YARD

As I complained loudly about an election a few years ago, Dale Helm, one of Ovilla's upstanding citizens, explained American voters to me. "Unless something is happening in their front yards, people just don't give a damn," he said.

That answered my question about why so many people continued to elect a man that we had campaigned so hard against. Despite our attempt to inform all voters about his highly questionable actions and his continual stretching of the truth, he kept winning elections.

Helm's statement came after I'd told several people about the scalawag's antics, each of whom responded, "I didn't know that!" That answer seemed odd since I personally had hung a two-page letter on each of their doors outlining his well-documented faults. Helm was right; none of them had bombs in their front yards, nor threats of City incursion on their property, nor elevated taxes or water costs. Since it wasn't in their front yards, they didn't register any of the important facts in their data banks.

Our claims were upheld when the City Council heard formal complaints filed by two different people against the Mayor. A unanimous vote found him guilty of 32 different violations of the Code of Ethics, the code he'd helped write. He could hardly claim he didn't understand them, now could he? Unfortunately, the City Council has no power to punish offenders; their only option is to publicly censure them for their actions. They did censure him and the newspapers had a heyday. Our problem politician resigned a week or so later.

We were elated that justice had prevailed, after a fashion, but were concerned by a report that he had said: "In two years nobody will remember any of this." He was gone, but was he gone for good?

We got our answer exactly two years later when he declared as a candidate for the office of the retiring Commissioner of Ellis County Precinct 4. Fortunately, some of us remembered his record; a number of residents of our city wrote letters to the editors of multiple newspapers, as did mayors of surrounding municipalities.

Then, one talented person built an impressive website that listed all of the ethics charges against the candidate along with copies of the public documents proving the charges. It listed all of his transgressions, documented with public documents, yet he insisted they were false charges made by a few malcontents.

I'll say this for him, he spent money like there was no tomorrow. Everywhere you looked, there was one of his ugly, black 4'X6' campaign signs. When workers saw some appear on property of voters who publicly supported his opponent, they notified the landowners who immediately removed the signs planted without permission.

To illustrate his devious mind, the candidate attempted to use his bad behavior to his advantage. He publicly claimed that his opponent's supporters had stolen his signs and T-posts.

I obtained copies of all his (and his opponent's) Campaign Finance Reports, primarily to see how much he spent and who had given him money. I was surprised to see how much he'd spent, much more than one would expect for a little county race. Most surprising, he'd spent $17,000 more than he'd taken in. That means his wallet was much lighter than before.

That seems fair to me. The man cost dedicated campaign workers a lot of time and money to defeat a person with no qualifications. Unfortunately, anybody in America can run for an office whether he knows anything about the job or not. If he can fool enough voters, he gets the job. Luckily, the aforementioned politician didn't get close to winning, despite fooling a lot of people. It bothers me when a person with a well-documented bad reputation survives a primary and makes it to a run-off election. That does more than bother me, folks; it scares me!

I like to think I've mellowed with age, learning to tolerate people who disagree with me – or at least bite my tongue in silence. Things that still infuriate me, however, are lying and cheating. No politician who adopts either of these traits deserves election to any office.

I hope more voters start looking beyond their front yards.

MORE THAN ONE BOSS BITCH

After our two long-lived Brittany spaniels died, we were left with the cocker spaniel Bettie's boss had convinced her to take off his hands as company for our aging bird dog. Pumpkin was a beautiful specimen with luxurious ears – and indefatigable energy. She chased birds, dug lawns, fought water sprinklers – Pumpkin could do everything but lie quietly. Her only downtime seemed to be naps on the king size bed with my bride.

Imagine Bettie's horror when she got home one afternoon to find the side gate broken and her Pumpkin missing! She was inconsolable. She got worse after a good Samaritan called to tell us he'd heard our alarm go off as he drove past our house. He saw a Mexican man with an orange dog in his arms running toward a car, but by the time he got turned around, car, dog and thief were gone.

I'd find her crying several times a day, wondering if someone was mistreating her baby. Not knowing was terrible! So, I immediately painted a 4'X8' sign (in Spanish) offering $100 for information leading to Pumpkin's return, a nice reward for 1987. We also posted ads in the morning paper, a fiasco that led to visits ending with an explanation that a cocker spaniel looked nothing like a Doberman/Chihuahua/Yorkie, etc. I didn't tell Bettie about the call from a woman who said she was a teacher whose class had found an orange Cocker dead beside a nearby schoolyard fence that matched Pumpkin's description.

I had given up by the time I got a call from a woman only a couple of miles from my workplace. I went by to check after work, but it wasn't Pumpkin. The lady proposed that I take the dog since she'd tried for weeks to find the owner; besides, the little Cocker was terrorizing her three Dobermans. She suggested I take it for my wife to consider as a replacement; she'd take the dog back if she didn't work out.

So, gullible me, I took the little fur ball home. She bounded into the house and wiggled all over when she saw Bettie. I left them alone in the bedroom for an hour or so – until my bride walked into the living room and announced with a smile, "We're keeping this one even if we find Pumpkin!"

Since she was a honey-colored ball of fur, we appropriately named her Honey Bear. She immediately took over the house and claimed it as her own. We also found we could have, just as appropriately, named her Chow Hound. The main thing was Bettie's recovery from the depression. It's hard to be sad and giggle at the antics of a dog at the same time.

Then came the phone call a week later from a couple who said they'd found our dog. She didn't have an owner's tag on her collar, but they located us through her rabies tag from our vet. They had watched our dog for a couple of weeks, saying that their Mexican apartment manager sent out workers every day. They suspected the workers burglarized houses for him. Pumpkin was one of a long line of dogs they'd brought him.

When the manager let her out one morning and went back inside, they lured her into their apartment. They found her tag and called the SPCA to find the vet's number; the vet gave them our phone number. The Mexican connection matched what the witness had told us, so I went to their apartment to check. It was our long-lost, supposed-to-be-dead Pumpkin! I gave the folks a $100 reward they didn't know about and took our kidnapped Cocker home.

I quickly dropped her over the gate into the back yard and went inside to spread the good news. I never considered that multiple females usually coexist only when one is firmly established as the boss, usually by being there first. So, when Bettie excitedly opened the back door, Honey Bear beat her out the door and we witnessed two bosses protecting their turf. When Pumpkin was stolen, she had been the lone inhabitant and boss lady. She came home to find an interloper. Likewise, Honey Bear had been the lone ruler until she discovered this strange invader in her yard that night.

My bride still remembers the duo with tears in her eyes; they complemented each other wonderfully and she loved them both. Pumpkin was beautiful, energetic and always busy; Honey Bear was quiet and lovable. She could have spent 22 hours a day sitting in Bettie's lap without complaint – that's 24 hours minus two hours for bathroom calls.

After several weeks of peacekeeping efforts, the dogs began to tolerate each other – a little. Oh, they slept peacefully curled into one tight ball, but both of them often bristled at mealtime. Pumpkin loved to lie off to one side watching her full food dish until Honey Bear finished hers and went for the full dish. The fight was on, every time. One or the other fastened an alligator grip on an ear of the other until we could inflict enough pinch-pain on an ear of the gripper to cause the release of the grippee.

So, they lived under an uneasy truce until Honey Bear passed away seven years later. During those years, moods ranged from playful to suspicious to all out violent. We had great times, but we never again forgot rule 32: one boss bitch per home.

My bride cuddles boss Honey Bear while
Pumpkin, the other boss, waits her turn

NO MORE MR. AMERICA COMPETITIONS

The only skin products on the market in the 1940s didn't block sun rays. Instead, they were tanning aids; use tanning cream to turn a person into a bronze Adonis – or Cleopatra, if you prefer. No one ever mentioned the "C" word – ever.

I remember meeting the dermatologist who invented and marketed Overcast 15, the first sunscreen I ever saw, at the Shooting, Hunting and Outdoor Trade Show in the late 1970s. Charly McTee and I attended the Overcast 15 seminar and were stunned by the photographs and data the doctor presented. When the doctor choked a bit at one point, he apologized and explained his emotion. The photo was of his grandfather's back. Despite admonitions to his family, his grandfather ignored warning signs too long and ultimately died of a melanoma.

One reason for the sizeable attendance at the presentation was free cancer screening for everyone. After a close examination of my face and shoulders, the doctor advised that I live in a closet for the rest of my life. My fair skin and light hazel eyes did not bode well for a life in the sun. Barring a lifetime in a closet, he advised that I NEVER go into the sun without sunscreen, whether his or someone else's product. He strongly recommended that I get a thorough annual examination by a dermatologist due to my history of sunburn and my outdoor lifestyle.

He made a believer out of me. Despite blistering three times a year throughout my youth, the doctor insisted using sunscreen is better late than never. So, I ordered Overcast 15 by the case as long as it was available and tried other brands when it ran out. I always lathered liberally with high octane protection anytime I went outside, even on cloudy days – make that **especially** on cloudy days.

I wasn't surprised when Dr. Bateman removed a suspicious spot from my forehead in 2006, nor when she called and said we should trim it a little deeper to be sure she had removed all of the basal cell carcinoma. After she found an even larger one on my left wrist six years later, I wondered what was coming next.

I didn't have long to wait. On March 5, 2013, Dr. Bateman took a biopsy from a purplish lump just above my left jawline. When she called back this time, she was already scheduling appointments for me, one with a surgeon to check lymph nodes and another surgeon to remove the melanoma. Yep, the bad boy.

The first surgery to remove and check the three lymph nodes fed by the tumor wasn't bad, especially since it showed the melanoma hadn't spread. There wasn't a lot of laughing and joking going on it the operating room, though. I asked if my incision would heal in time for me to go to the prom, but they just gave me the look – yeah, that one, the "You old fool!" look.

The surgery to remove the melanoma wasn't all that pleasant since it was done under local anesthetic. Oh, it didn't hurt, but the scratchy sound of the blade cutting through the tissue was a little unnerving, as was the smell of burning flesh when they cauterized the wound. But then they bandaged the incision and told me to come back in three hours. They would know then whether they had to take more and if so, how much and from where.

It was a lo-o-o-o-ong wait, but it ended beautifully. My knees got weak when the young lady called my name, but she smiled and told me it was totally contained and they'd removed all the cancer on the first try. It's a good thing she told me that right away; otherwise I'd have fainted when she gave me a mirror for a look at the results. It looked like someone had carved a deviled egg out of my cheek and painted it black.

I'll never forget the surgeon's words. He said, "We took a lot out, but luckily you've plenty of skin left." Then he explained how he would trim both ends to points (darts, I think Mom would call them) to keep the skin from bulging at the ends, pull the skin together and sew it up, from the inside out. I don't recommend it as the best way to get a facelift, but they pulled the wrinkles right out of that left side. Two plastic surgeons worked for an hour and a half pulling and tugging on the stitches as the doctor asked me questions about gardening. If his squash and tomatoes turned out as well as the surgery, he probably fed the entire neighborhood all summer.

When I got my first look at the five-inch, stitched incision, it resembled a tightly wrapped sausage about the diameter of a pencil. "It looks like I've lost my chance to ever win a Mr. America competition," I smiled.

He told me I'd be surprised in a couple of weeks, and I was. He took the stitches out a week later; two weeks after that it had faded into a thin white line. Now it's gone.

No one ever wants to hear the words melanoma, or cancer of any description, but if it's addressed early enough, chances are good it will turn out well. Just don't ever ignore an odd-looking spot – no matter how small. It could wipe out your last chance at a Mr. America title – or your life.

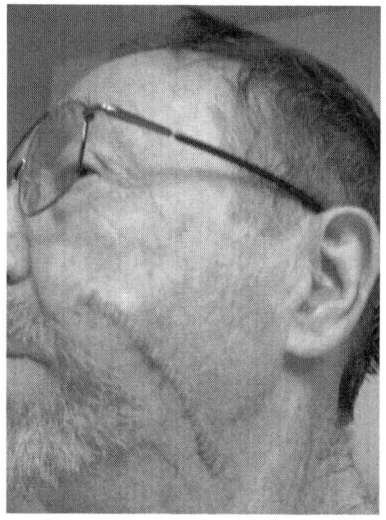

A next-day view after the excision of a melanoma that was only pea-sized on the surface

LETTERS VS. E-MAILS

It is no secret that I have railed from time to time about the ravages of progress. I don't want to do without electricity again, or give up indoor plumbing. I see no advantage to doing without either. Some of the new technology, though, I gladly do without. For example, I don't tweet; you twits can do it all you like, just don't try to make me do it.

I also have a computer – well, all right, three computers, but I have no desire to carry one around in my pocket. If folks can't wait until I get back to my computer, they can call me on that old-fashioned cell phone. Remember those? Mine still works very well, thank you, and I never rudely look away from anyone to watch an active computer screen in my hand. And even if a miracle cure comes along for arthritis, I won't text. I don't want to. Call me, dammit, and say, "Hello!" My thumbs can handle the "talk" and "end" buttons.

I've even mourned the loss of old-fashioned letters we used to communicate back in the old days. Imagine what might have happened if our founding fathers had e-mail instead of crow-quill pens. How many historical documents would have survived computer crashes? I lost many e-mails from several friends who went on ahead before e-mail storage improved. Now we have the capability to save, print, share, or whatever, our communications. For example, I found a copy of the first e-mail below in a drawer as I searched for another document. After finding the hard copy, I unearthed the original e-mail exchange which allowed me to relive the pleasure they brought back in 2011. I don't have them in our original handwriting, but the thoughts below are clear enough. Maybe I'll just use the things I like.

Oh, yeah, thank you again, Judi.

From: Judi Hogg
Date: March 31, 2011 10:02:14 PM EDT
To: *(MWHS Class of 1959)*

OK, now I know I am a book addict, but am selective in my reading material. I am and have been hooked on John Graves, Elmer Kelton,

Larry McMurtry, John Grisham, Lee Child, and on and on. But have found another favorite in Morris Gresham. I got his 2 books from Amazon yesterday and just switch back and forth between them whenever I have a few moments, like when the potatoes are cooking, loading the dishwasher one-handed, waiting at a stop light. I am very excited to go to the local market (Wally World) and get some ingredients so I don't have to stop and run get something once I get started.

Just want to thank whoever started this email for putting me on to him and Bettie Carolyn - I think she may have gone to high school in Millsap with my husband. And I do take care of my books, no pages turned down, no pages flattened out along the spine, etc. My daughter loves to read also and I will have some good books to leave her.

And another coincidence, I have found, is that my daughter lives in Red Oak, just a hop - skip - jump away from Ovilla. They moved over there about 10 years ago when she went to work in the corporate office of a brick conglomerate - Hanson Brick. But her husband lived in the Acme Brick housing when he was a kid at Bennett. Says that when a larger house became empty, they just up and moved to that one. Think his father drove trucks for Acme and was killed in an accident when he was about 5 or 6.

I am ready to go to bed now with a book to read until my eyes fall shut (Lee Child is by the bed, Morris Gresham is by the couch in the den and Nicklas Sparks is in the car for when I have a few minutes when we are out and about).

Thanks again and happy reading.

Judi Hogg

On Apr 4, 2011, at 3:07 PM, Morris Gresham wrote:

Judi, Judi, Judi (in a Cary Grant accent, of course):
(The Devil made me do that!)

I was blown away by your e-mail to the Class of 1959. I told Bettie that I should try to hire you as my agent! You were overly kind -- and I LOVED it! Especially humbling was being mentioned in the same sentence with John Graves whom I've met and respect and with Elmer Kelton who had attended our Texas Outdoor Writers Association meetings and was a friend until his death last year. He was, I think, the one writer who wrote about **my** life. His stories, in fact, goaded me into collecting our family stories which ultimately became my two books. I'm about half finished with the third. Thank you so much for your kind words.

You are correct in that Jack went to school with Bettie at Millsap. She was a star basketball player down there. I knew Jack back then as well and we saw both of y'all (I think) back in 2007 when you opened the shop full of mementoes across from the Baker Hotel for our Class of 1958 to browse through. Jack also knew my mother-in-law's boyfriend Deen Porter who worked in a warehouse out at Wolters. It's a small world!

At my age I have trouble remembering who's on the other line, much less who married whom, but if you were in the Class of 1959, you must be Judi Plowman, the only Junior in the *1958 Burro* spelled "Judi". If you are, then I remember you as well. (Bad memory or not, I remember damned near every pretty girl!)

If I don't know your son-in-law's father, I'll bet my Dad did. What are the names? Your daughter probably lives within five or six miles of us. We live one mile north of Ovilla City Hall and exactly five miles from the Ovilla Road (Texas 664) - I-35 intersection. Our favorite restaurant is Amaya's Bar and Grill on 342 in Red Oak.

Thank you again for your kind words. You help make the work worthwhile. Hope to see you sometime.

Best,
Morris Gresham

Photo evidence that it is, indeed, a small world: Judi Hogg's daughter's father-in-law is the late Glen Walker, the young man holding the bat in this Henderson Family photo of 1945. My bride is the young lady holding the other bat. Glen's sister Lorraine, far left, stands next to his brother Leo; his brother Lawson is at the far right. Jim Nevil, the gent kneeling with his baby son Ray, was my father-in-law and the person who gave Glen his lifelong nickname, Cobb. Small world, ain't it?

From: Judi Hogg
Apr 4, 2011

Thanks for taking time from retirement to respond. I was Judi Plowman, sister to Kermit. Had lunch with him today and showed him the part about your poker party at our family log house at bottom of Millsap Mountain. He grinned and reminded me he had bad reputation then. (He didn't need to remind me.) I came along the next year and teachers asked if I was like him. Fortunately, people do grow up and he just retired from being computer consultant for Dallas County Community College.

I showed Linda Butler your book at church yesterday and had to use force to get it back.

Went to store after church and got big batch of turnip greens, salt pork & turnips and smelled them cooking all afternoon. lol.

Looking forward to your next book. I know of 4 who are buying your books as we speak. Hurry and finish next one!

Judi, Judi, Judi

Sent from my iPhone

WHAT IF IT STOPS?

I've been around a while now, selling words in magazines, newspapers and books. I remembered being surprised back in 1974 when I made my first sale. At age 34, I discovered that people actually paid for words I put on paper – and not words that I had invented; I merely arranged them.

That sale was just the first in a lifetime of good fortune. I submitted manuscripts to a wide variety of publishers over a forty year period with only one rejection letter – and I promptly sold that rejected manuscript to a competing publication. The longer I wrote, the easier it got, but I can't tell you why.

I remember marveling at the skill of a piano player at our Lake Navarro Mills hoedowns a decade ago. T.W. could join any song after a couple of bars, whether he'd ever heard it or not, and never miss a note. He could sound like Floyd Cramer or Liberace or anyone else you could name. Once I asked T. how he did it; I'll never forget his answer. "I never had any lessons and I don't read music," he said. "I don't think about it; the music just comes out the ends of my fingers."

I couldn't comprehend how such a thing could happen at the time, but I think I understand it now.

The last couple of years, folks have become more and more complimentary of my work. It's kind of embarrassing for a shy country boy; I still think they are too kind. More and more often, though, I re-read things I had written and wondered how I wrote them, if I had.

I remember receiving a magazine a few years ago that contained a story I had written. As I read the first few paragraphs, drastic changes the editor had made to my work shocked me. I went to my loose leaf notebooks of manuscripts (this was the pre-computer era) and retrieved the story I had submitted four months earlier. When I compared the original to the magazine version, I was shocked to see the editor hadn't changed a word – not one word!

Similar things kept happening and I often look at a line I've just typed and think, "Did I write that?" It became apparent to me that I really had no control over my writing. Like T.W.'s notes, my words seem to jump from my fingertips onto the screen. I know I'll catch flak for that last statement, but fact is fact. Oh, I edit everything I write, but usually just grammar, spelling or the order of words, not the concept or the original thought string.

One night as good friend Pamela Woodall visited in our home, she read an essay I'd just written. She pointed to one sentence she particularly liked and asked how I figured out which words to use. I told her I had no idea how it happened, that words just seem to appear by themselves.

"It's a God-given talent," Pam asserted.

"It probably is, since **all** things come from God," I said, "but it bothers me that I seem to have no control over what comes out of my mind."

"But that's a good thing," she said.

"Maybe it is," I admitted, "but since I have no control over it, what if it stops? What if the words quit coming?"

"Oh, they're never going to stop," Pam insisted.

Lord, I hope she's right. As I wrote in my second book, I told my mother once that I couldn't figure out what I had done to deserve God being so good to me. Why had He allowed me, just an average country boy with no college education, to enjoy success as a mechanical engineer and manager while working at the same time as a freelance writer and as an editor for state, regional and national magazines?

With the wisdom available only to Christian mothers, she replied, "Maybe He just hasn't told you what He wants from you yet."

Today my receiving is even further ahead of my giving; since Mom went away, I've had continued financial success and won state and national awards for writing – and this is my fourth book since then. I suppose I should say **His** fourth book...

When He finally tells me what he wants for payback, I bet it's a doozy. Whatever it is, I'll consider it more than a fair trade for the blessings I received.

FIVE FOOT EIGHTEEN

Old friend and co-worker Kenneth Gasch is a highly visible individual, an obvious result of his 6'-6" stature. In answer to inevitable questions about his height, he **always** says, "Five foot eighteen."

I was delighted when Gasch and I became the first two employees Dr. Jimmy Rogers took with him from Continental Electronics to the Superconducting Super Collider. Dr. Rogers, Vice President of Engineering at Continental, headed the RF Group of the Accelerator Division of the Super Collider. Gasch, an electrical technician, was tasked with setting up the test lab for our group.

Gasch was not just proficient in his job; he performed those duties in a lighthearted manner. Not everyone, however, was impressed. I'll never forget one government-mandated training session all employees attended, Sexual Harassment Awareness Training it was called.

A very competent (I suppose) young lady lectured us about what we could do and could not do. In 1990, when the world was just beginning to talk about sexual harassment, government-funded employers wanted to avoid any legal problems; hence, we were taught how to act like ladies and gentlemen.

Our trainer explained that if a person told another person to stop any action that offended him/her, whether a statement or action, a failure to stop at that point would constitute sexual harassment. Gasch raised his hand with a question for our trainer, "So, if I say something a woman doesn't like, but I stop when she tells me to stop, that's all right?"

"Yes," the trainer answered.

"Then that means I get one free shot at everybody?"

Whether it was a couple of hundred folks erupting in laughter or her suspicion that Gasch might be serious, our trainer went ballistic. She ranted at him and at the entire room, reminding us that sexual harassment was not a joking matter. Also, her complaints to the highest officials filtered quickly down to Dr. Rogers who suggested that Gasch might avoid jokes in the future during public interactions at official functions.

Of course, Gasch had fun whether it was public or not. I remember the day our secretary berated Gasch for buying that cheap Hills Bros. coffee for our group coffee pool. She insisted that he stick to proven brands like Folgers or Maxwell House. So, Gasch dutifully removed all offending coffee. He poured all the Hills Bros. coffee into Folger's cans and brought them back to the lab.

When our secretary tasted her first cup after noting the Folger's cans, she proclaimed, "This is the way coffee is supposed to taste."

She drank that cheap coffee for three more years without ever suspecting her taste had been compromised.

Gasch's jokes even infected his unsuspecting co-workers. When workers began setting up the buildings at our new Waxahachie location to get us out of the converted warehouses in DeSoto, Gasch preceded the rest of our group to oversee construction of various elements of our test lab. There were no offices or telephones there except for the operators at the front entry desk. When it was necessary to contact Gasch, we left a message for him with the operator.

One day we couldn't raise Gasch on his cell phone, a frequent occurrence in a building loaded with electrical interference, I called the Waxahachie operator. "If you see Gasch or can get a message to him, tell him to call as soon as possible. Tell him it's an immer jincey."

"Immer jincey?" she questioned. "Can you spell that?"

"Sure," I said. "It's E-M-E-R-G-E-N-C-Y. Got it?

"Yes, I have it, thank you."

"Read it back to me," I said.

"Immer ... Oh! You! ....*click*"

It was OK, though; she blamed Gasch....

SOME VIPS ARE IMPORTANT, SOME AIN'T

We've had some historic events in Texas, but when Johnny Morris opened his first Texas store at Grapevine, Texas on March 26, 1999, now, that was a big deal, right up there with the Texas Centennial in 1936. It was big enough to lure young Kendal Hemphill from the hinterlands of Mason, Texas to the humongous Metroplex.

When the young outdoor writer called to see if I was going the Grand Opening ceremonies for the new Bass Pro Shops location, my confirmation led him to ask if my long-standing offer to put him up in our Ovilla digs still stood. Kendal was concerned about finding his way around the big city alone, living as he did in a small town with one blinking light.

He found his way to our home all right since he only had to make two turns after leaving Highway 67 – but he was an hour late. His volunteer fireman soul prompted him to help fight a house fire he saw coming through Dublin. Then we lost a little more time while he showered to wash away the smokehouse smell. Luckily, I was a regular Mario Andretti in those days; we made it to the store early enough to make it to the VIP section before the festivities began.

We found old friend Paul Cañada already entrenched behind the yellow ribbon marking the VIP area along the entry path to the stage. Jerry Jones was there, but no one paid him any attention; at that time he was just the fellow who fired Tom Landry. As Kendal chatted with Cañada, the first VIP walked past. "There's George W. Bush," I said. Kendal glanced around and kept talking.

"Here comes Porter Wagoner," I told my bride. Kendal merely glanced around briefly again and kept talking.

There's Jeannie Pruitt," I told my bride. Kendal didn't even look around.

"Who's that over there by Little Jimmy Dickens?" my bride asked.

"Oh, that's Bobby Bare," I answered.

"Where?" Kendal asked, as he spun around and came to full attention. "Where is he? Bobby Bare has been my favorite singer since I was in high school. I learned every song he ever sang!"

"He's right over there," I said, pointing toward a trio of stars about 20 yards from us. "Would you like to meet him?"

"How would I meet him? He'd never talk to me," Kendal said.

With that, I raised my arm, snapped my fingers and called, "Bobby!" When he looked toward us, I called, "Over here!" and gave him a come-here wave. I'm fairly certain that Kendal's breathing stopped as Bare sauntered toward us.

As I shook Bare's hand, I said, "This is Kendal Hemphill, an outdoor writer from Mason, Texas. He knows every one of your songs; he's your number one fan and he's dying to meet you."

The hero worship was evident as they shook hands and talked for a few minutes. When Bare left to join the others on stage, Kendal asked me how I'd known he would talk to us. "I didn't know," I admitted, "but you never know unless you ask."

"Well, that's been a few years ago," Kendal admitted when I recently reminded him of that event. "But then, time doesn't mean what it used to. I do remember Bare asking me what my favorite song of his was. I told him, 'The Maremaid.' He never said mermaid. He said maremaid. And he said, 'But you didn't like the tail.'

"That was a lot of fun," Kendal continued. "Paul *(Cañada)* tried to get me in trouble. He said, 'Go over to that big guy with the nice suit and the wire in his ear and give him a wedgie.' Bush had some security there, you know.

"Paul kept going out and taking pictures during the speeches," Kendal remembered. "I asked him how many he was going to take. He said, 'I'm not taking pictures, I'm just blocking Jerry Jones's view.' Good times."

Yes, they were.

After the formal festivities ended, we wandered slowly through the spotlessly new and spectacular showplace, gawking and talking as we went. By the time we spotted Johnny Morris standing in an aisle, Kendal was no longer star struck. I had met Johnny several times when I was editor of the magazine raising much of the money used to build the Texas Freshwater Fisheries Center in Athens. My photos of him and his son appeared on our magazine covers as well as interior layouts.

"C'mon," I said. "Let me introduce you to Johnny."

I shook hands with the owner of Bass Pro Shops and introduced the two; then Kendal took over.

"This is a fantastic store, Mr. Morris! I know it will do well," he said, "but I was just thinking. I'll bet if you built one of these in Mason, Texas, where I live, folks would come from all over to buy things. I know it would be successful! We've only got one blinking light, so traffic wouldn't be a problem."

Throughout this speech, Johnny Morris looked from Kendal to me, back to Kendal and back to me again with a helpless, unbelieving look that asked, "Who is this guy?" He wasn't sure if the writer with the Texas accent was serious or not. He still doesn't know. Did I mention that Kendal is an award winning writer of outdoor humor, among other things?

Kendal never got his Bass Pro Shops in Mason, but they built one just down the road on the north side of San Antonio. That'll have to do…

FROM THE FRYING PAN INTO THE FIRE

If nothing else, my engineering life was varied – from time to time. I toiled on mechanical designs for antenna systems, high-power radar and communication transmitters, RF equipment for an atom smasher, vehicle-towed portable power converters used to power parked airplanes, high-speed mail sorting machines, conveyor systems and, finally, the engine used to tow cars in an automated rail-car/conveyor system.

I'll admit the challenge of designing a mini-choo-choo engine was fun; the company was not. My boss told me the company did not allow unpaid leaves of absence; if they needed you at all, they needed you all the time. Before I accepted the job, he never mentioned that policy which would spell the end of my long-time job as the Skeet Shooting World Championships reporter for *The Skeet Shooting Review*. Since Siemens Electrocom had allowed me the time off a month after my employment began, by pre-employment agreement, I assumed it would be allowed every year.

Rule 19: never assume.

A hectic week of 15-hour work days and multiple drives to San Antonio, managed to satisfy both employers' requirements; they got what they paid for with major loss of sleep and mileage for a harried engineer/outdoor writer. That experience, however, convinced me I didn't belong at a company with such inflexible rules. I decided quickly and within a month, I'd jumped right out of that frying pan.

I began to worry about the new flames within a week of beginning a job with Currency Systems International to design elements of high-speed currency handling machines. Actually, the tinder was smoking before I began my labors, while I was still attending the school to learn Pro Engineer, the solid modeling software used at CSI.

It was an exciting time for a dinosaur who toiled through the parallel bar era, then drafting machines and, finally, AutoCAD computer programs to generate drawings. This new concept of generating solid models of a part, then assembling it into its next assembly to assure fit was beyond cool. Once the part was generated, the program generated the drawing, reading the dimensions right from the part. No muss, no fuss, no errors!

Then a telephone call from my boss, the Manager of Mechanical Engineering, delayed the use of my new-found design knowledge. First, CSI wanted me to travel to the U.K. for three weeks to solve a problem with parts designed and built by a British supplier. Never mind that I'd never seen one of CSI's sorters, much less operate one, my boss said. They wanted fresh eyes on the problem. Besides, a young CSI engineer had been working for three months to eliminate the reasons for failing the acceptance test by Barclay's Bank in Manchester; he needed a trip home to see his family. I'd have the two weeks until the next acceptance test to fix the problems.

The young engineer collected me, as the Brits would say, at the Manchester Airport and drove me to the little town of Crewe and the offices of Manchester Machine & Design, our partner in the project. CSI built the basic sorter; MMD designed and manufactured the accessories – the stackers and the bundler. A feeder mechanism fed banknotes into the machine which sorted the currency by denomination and deposited notes into the proper pocket. A strapper wrapped a band around a selected number of notes and printed a barcode on the strap. When scanned, the barcode revealed the serial number of each note in the strap.

This strap then fell into the stacker before being conveyed to a bundler which wrapped the straps into bundles with another barcode. The problem, I was told, was seven failures during the acceptance test at the transition from CSI's strapper to the MMD stacker.

After meeting management and engineering personnel, I was introduced to the problem machinery. The young CSI engineer explained the seven problems by showing me seven stackers with his recommendation for seven different changes to fix the problems – a different fix for each problem. Then he went home to Mama, leaving a slightly worried newbie behind. I didn't think a different configuration for every stacker was a good idea, but I was the new guy. Let's have a look.

They bundled me off to Abingdon, a little town just south of Oxford, armed with a couple of high-speed video cameras, and in the company of software engineer Tony King, a nice chap who could run our machine at the CSI Abingdon facility. I had been told we'd have real English pounds to run my tests, but U.K. bankers (or insurers) ix-nayed sending a million pounds to CSI's low security facility. So, we spent the first couple of hours beating up stacks of brand new test notes – and it takes a lot of twisting, stomping and ruffling to turn fake currency into anything resembling real money.

When we finally began running the test notes, I saw the first failure within a few minutes – before we ever set up the cameras. Then, a couple of minutes later, we saw the second failure, a different one. Within an hour, we identified all seven failures and they all began at the same point, at a lip on the flapper plate that dropped the strapped notes into the stacker. We kept running and saw the failures occur again and again.

So, I removed the flapper and flattened the lip with a hammer. Then I changed the bend line of the lip by 10 degrees or so and used a vise and hammer to bend the lip at a different angle. You have no idea how happy this country boy was after we ran four hours straight without another failure. We beat a path back to Crewe with our newly hammered plate and the revisions began.

A couple of days later, we delivered the upgraded machine to Barclays Bank in Manchester and, after enduring a series of checks which fell just short of cavity searches, we got into the bank. We tried to ignore the millions of pounds of real money stacked all around us as we began the acceptance test. You know, there really is a smell of money; 20-pound notes don't smell like newspaper, nor do they look like comic strips. But a few short hours later, I walked out of Barclays after a perfect performance by all of the CSI and MMD machinery. Then I slept the sleep of the righteous before an early morning flight home.

I didn't return a hero, exactly, but all the big shots knew my name after that. The fire hadn't been as bad as the frying pan after all…

IT AIN'T FAKE!

"It ain't fake" was my grandpa Tom Emberlin's retort to anyone ridiculing Saturday Night Wrestling in the 1950s and '60s. He, like many oldsters, stayed up past the news that one night a week just to watch the good guys battle the forces of evil. I remember the early sixties, when I'd come into Pasadena Heights Baptist Church on Sunday morning. As I'd bend to kiss my grandmother, Mama Minnie Gresham, she'd invariably ask, "Did you see Keomuka get beat last night?" She and her sister, my great-aunt Lena Weldon, never missed rasslin' and they loved to see perennial bad guy Duke Keomuka get his just desserts.

I remember a few of the names. Fritz von Erich began as a villain but later morphed into a good guy as he wielded his famous "iron claw." He fathered sons who carried on the Von Erich dynasty on into the '80s, but tragic deaths claimed several of the boys.

Then there were midget wrestlers as well as Slave Girl Moolah and Daisy Mae, two "lady" wrestlers, that Pa loved to watch. They appeared once at a wrestling extravaganza at the Mineral Wells Convention Center, I think that old red brick building was called. I drove Pa to the matches and sat through the choreographed moves, watching him rail at referees who failed to catch cheating moves by villains.

After the matches, we drove past a big sedan on the street behind the building and saw a laughing Slave Girl Moolah and Daisy Mae climb into the back seat of the car together, seemingly no longer interested in killing each other. Pa got terribly angry when I asked, "Still think it's not fake?" He was so mad that the incident was never mentioned again – until now. Sorry, Pa, but it WAS fake.

When I began my last engineering job at CSI, I met a young designer there named Jimmy Everett. One day someone mentioned wrestling and I told a couple of funnies about my Pa. Jimmy told me that his grandmother had attended the events at the old Sportatorium and sat in the front row every Saturday night. Then he told about her blowing a referee's whistle when a villain did anything to cheat.

I remembered her! We'd get tickled when a wrestler pulled something from the top of his trunks to hit his opponent. She'd blow that whistle so loud we could hear it above the announcers' voices and the crowd noise. She was just a tiny thing from the same mold as Granny Clampett, but those brutes didn't scare her! Jimmy and I shared many stories about our grandparents' addiction to rasslin'.

Daddy used to make fun of Pa for watching wrestling, but we all noticed he was always there "keeping Pa company." But it didn't surprise anyone when Daddy kept staying up for wrestling after Pa was gone. I stayed up with him sometimes just to watch him squirm on the couch when one of his favorites would get caught in a bad hold. I never learned to enjoy wrestling, but I got a kick out of watching Daddy enjoy it. Good times…

After writing the previous paragraphs last evening, I opened the paper this morning to big wrestling news. The headlines announced WWE's WrestleMania 32 is scheduled for AT&T Stadium in Arlington in 2016. They expect a new attendance record, and they will probably reach it, but the big shock to me was a statement made by WWE CEO Vince McMahon.

"It's not pro wrestling," said McMahon. "We're entertainers. This is a vast experience of the soap opera and the theatre of what we put on. You're not going to find anything in the world that has more grandeur than this."

The newspaper reported that officials readily admit the wrestling is scripted and the winners are predetermined. Fans watch it, they say, for the same reason people watch plays or movies – to be carried away by the stories.

I read those words with my own eyes, but it's hard for me to believe they finally admitted it in print! I'm glad Mama and Pa never had their dreams dashed by such public statements; and I hope the buzzing noise in my head is tinnitus from my shooting days and not the sound of them spinning in their graves…

GASTRONOMIC REVELATIONS

As a dyed-in-the-wool country boy, I've eaten things that don't appear in French restaurants, liking some, hating others. I have also tried food that ritzy folks call delicacies. I disliked many of them. I'm a firm believer that taste is a matter of free choice; however, I'm not sure I'll ever trust someone who dislikes okra – but that's just me…

I've eaten some wonderful seafood platters in my day, the best at Papadeaux and the old Zuider Zee on Denton Drive in Dallas. They included delicious items such as fried shrimp, fried oysters, fried fish, stuffed crab and maybe crawdads… well, city folk call 'em crawfish. Of course, that table top covered with seafood at the Boiling Pot in Rockport, Texas is incomparable!

A platter I ate (partially) in the city of Paphos on the island of Cyprus, however, was yucky, to use a word understood by my nieces and nephews. I know the platter had several critters I liked well enough to eat, but the only one I remember liking was the barbecued squid. It wasn't bad. The two things I couldn't tolerate were the fried minnows and the octopus. I think they called the little fried crispy critters some kind of fish, but they were minnows, no doubt about it. I've caught crappie on bigger minnows.

First off, I don't eat critters that haven't been gutted; don't want to, don't have to. Besides, the fried minnows also had all of their shiny little scales and all bones and fins. I was told to just chew them well and I wouldn't even notice the crisp bones. I didn't because you can't get a bone in your throat if you don't put it into your mouth. Case closed!

The octopus, now, I tried; I really did. The chunk of leg I chewed for a couple of hours was off a trophy ink spitter. The hollow leg was probably three-quarters of an inch in diameter and the suction cup was one-half inch or larger. I don't know how this thing was cooked, if it WAS cooked, but I didn't damage it a lick while tiring my jaws to exhaustion. And since I refused to swallow it whole, I still have never eaten Cyprus octopus.

I did eat some memorable meals on the island, though. My favorite was porterhouse steak and shrimp cocktail. The porterhouses were probably an inch or inch and a quarter thick and cooked perfectly. And the shrimp were HUGE and delicious. I'll wager those live shrimp looked more like immature lobsters, but not too young at that. We ate those steaks in local restaurants around the town of Akrotiri. We always drank Keo beer with our food (or without food), but not many. Keo was bottled only in quart bottles and it was high-octane, none of that light stuff. The Brits were still serving their beer lukewarm at that time, but not the Cypriots. They served it cold, cold, cold! And it was great!

We ate most of our meals at the Officers Mess on the UK Military Installation. Their breakfasts were great. A full English breakfast would fit well on Texas farms – well, almost. We don't eat roasted to-mah-tos for breakfast here, but I loved them. I also liked the baked beans, but my bride still shoots me a funny look when I mention the baked beans on English breakfasts.

I also love English sausages; Mike Still, a hunting buddy of the English persuasion, told me they called them "chubbies." So, I had chubbies, roasted tomatoes, baked beans, scrambled eggs, toast and marmalade every morning – and lots of it. Lots of it because I knew I wouldn't be crazy about the other meals. They weren't bad, necessarily, but the Brits of 1985 just didn't cook by Texas farm boy rules. They seem to love roasted potatoes and they ruined them in a variety of ways. The most common roasted potato was burned on the outside and raw in the middle. And those were the better ones!

Also, I was slightly embarrassed after asking a waiter when he was serving the Yorkshire pudding I'd ordered; he told me I'd already eaten it. It wasn't pudding at all, but a pastry that looked mightily like a sopapilla. Why don't they call it Yorkshire pastry? Can't they speak English? Oh, well.

When I returned to the U.K. in the late '90s, the food was highly improved – and the beer was noticeably colder. Tony King told me the old timers there hated cold beer, but the youngsters demanded it. One reason the food improved, I think, is that we ate pub food almost exclusively.

One of the best meals I ever had there was the roast pork with vegetables I ordered one Sunday at a small town pub near Oxford. In fact, I told the server that my mother had fed a family of five on less food than I had on my platter. She was back in a flash and said,

"Cook says does that mean you'll be paying the price for five?" They didn't charge me for five, but maybe they should have; I ate it all and, as my Daddy would say, I sopped the gravy with those English rolls.

I guess you could say I have a love-hate relationship with British food. Actually, the only thing I hate are those damnable roasted potatoes. If they'd just learn to wrap them in foil and bake them! If you've ever been in a pub in the U.K. and didn't eat a sausage sandwich, I recommend that you never commit that sin again. I don't care who claims to have invented sausage, the Polish, Italians, Germans or Frenchies, the Brits have raised it right up there on a taste level with Tex-Mex nachos. Really!

I wish I could tell you how great kidney pie tastes, but I draw the line at some things. I don't eat food processing parts any further south than the liver. Well, there were those calf fries that time, but the open bar compromised a bunch of us; same thing with the turkey fries. But I can guarantee you they were delicious compared to suction cups...

I have eaten a couple of things, on purpose, that I won't be eating again. A couple of hunters I wanted to interview about Montana bear hunting scheduled a meeting at their favorite restaurant in Ft. Worth. They ordered a dozen escargot, but they couldn't fool me; those darned things were snails! I ate one and found it much like the rubber soles on U.S. Keds tennies. I did swallow it, so I officially ate a snail, but I didn't have to like it – and I didn't.

When they offered me another, I politely declined and they couldn't believe I didn't want more. I explained quite gently that they obvious had an erotic relationship with escargot (I said the word just to show them I could) and I don't; therefore, I'd stick to dipping the garlic bread into the delicious butter used to bake the snails.

The o'possum Aunt Nell tossed onto the roof to cure overnight before she baked it with sweet potatoes for me and Jimmy Floyd Tuggle was much better than the snail. The possum was a little greasy and the red color didn't look too great, but I et some; yes I did. It was all right, maybe, but if I ever see a possum in my headlights, it's committing suicide for no reason. I won't be cooking it -- or eating it. Jimmy Floyd can have 'em all...

Texas Outdoor Writer Bink Grimes and my bride Bettie enjoy one of the world's gastronomical delights, The Boiling Pot in Rockport, Texas.

DELUSIONS OF GRANDEUR

It's tough going through life with a tendency toward addictions. Tendency, my foot; I get addicted to anything I try once, if I like it. That's the way it's always been – baseball, smoking, girls, golf, bowling, fishing, hunting, writing and skeet shooting, to name the most addictive. I'm so glad I didn't smell a marijuana cigarette for the first time until the age of 58; if I'd smelled it at a younger age, I might have tried one and become a pot head. Whew! If I'd been that lucky with tobacco, it wouldn't have taken me 39 years to break an expensive and debilitating habit.

Baby Sister once complained to my mother that I was a perfectionist. Well, Mom spilled the beans and I fired back: if there are two ways to do something, I see absolutely no reason to do it the wrong way. OK, OK, maybe I've gotten a little obsessed from time to time about doing things the right way more times than anyone else. I still don't see anything wrong with wanting to kill the first deer, the largest deer and the most deer. If you're going to do it, excel at it, I say. Of course, the older I get, the more I excel at watching.

It only took a year or so to cure me of golf. I tried a round and thought how wonderful it would be to become a par golfer. So I bought some clubs and all the gear I could afford and hit the links several times a week after work. Then Jim Pratt and I would play some course or other a couple of weekends a month, usually 36 holes on Saturday and 27 on Sunday. No matter how much I practiced, I never could break 91. If I shot a 45 on the front, I shot 46 on the back. A 46 on the front made me hustle to make the 45 on the back.

Then there was the magical Saturday when Jim took me to a country club in Longview. I was hotter than a potbellied stove, finishing with 32 on the front nine. That's FOUR under par, for Pete's sake! I'd finally figured it out!

Then we started the back nine. I was out of bounds twice and in the water twice. And I finished with – a drum roll, please – a 59. Those of you who bothered to add the scores discovered that I still haven't broken a 91. Yep, 32 plus 59 equals 91, a good basketball score, but nothing more than an embarrassing round of golf.

Barbara Pratt was my bride's Matron of Honor and her husband Jim was my Best Man. He was with me when I started golfing and he was with me that last horrible day when I gave it up forever. Jim was a slower learner, though; he kept at it.

I can take a hint; I put the clubs in my closet until Roy McDonald asked me once if I had a set he could borrow for a company tournament. I kissed his hand and thanked him for taking the cursed tools out of my sight. I was already rolling some good bowling scores and I could do that on weeknights, leaving the weekends open for hunting and fishing. What had I been thinking anyway, wasting all that time on golf?

As my bowling averages climbed, I began to wonder how hard it would be to reach pro status. Oops, delusions of grandeur again. After my averages climbed higher and higher, I placed sixth in my division in the Dallas Match Games Championships. So, true to my addictions, I bowled more – and then more – and then some more.

Then I was told that all one had to do to gain membership in the Professional Bowlers Association was to average over 190 in three leagues and be sponsored by a PBA member. Heck, I already knew three PBA members and was averaging 189 in one league. That's close, right?

The next year I bowled in five leagues in four nights, with a low average of 193 and a high of 196. So I was in, right? Wrong! In a

Bronco Bowl classic league, my 193 average beat only three women and one man. Women? Yep, it was a mixed league and 13 of the 16 women carried a higher average than I did. How could I ever consider putting up a $200 entry fee to bowl against men when I couldn't even beat their women? The answer: I didn't; I dropped back to one league a week and enjoyed it a lot more – until skeet shooting came along.

    Unfortunately, I had a similar experience with skeet shooting; I loved it after shooting my first round and wanted to get as good at it as I could. So, through the years I bought better guns, bought more shot shell reloaders and shot more rounds of skeet. When I began practicing with world class shooters, I wanted to achieve their level of competence.

    Then I was tapped to cover the World Championships of Skeet for the *Skeet Shooting Review* and discovered that I had been harboring delusions of grandeur again. I watched three shooters break 550 targets, including 100 with the tiny .410, without a miss. A few more missed one out of the 550 and a dozen or so others dropped only two or three targets. I finally admitted that I didn't have the three ingredients needed to reach that level. I never had the time and the money and the desire all at the same time. And you've got to have all three and work harder than you ever worked at any job in your life. Just a few years ago I belonged to two gun clubs and shot 20 to 25 boxes of shells every week. Now I just try to remember where I store the Beretta 687 EELL tube set, not that I could carry the case any distance, much less swing the gun.

    Don't think that I've lost my competitive edge, though. I can still cut, split and stack more wood in a day than any other arthritic old coot in his mid-seventies – and that ain't a delusion…is it?

PAY IT FORWARD

Rude drivers bully their way dangerously into the lanes of careful folks, brutes jump line in grocery stores and otherwise sane individuals veer into the lane beside a driver moving at the same speed, effectively disrupting the normal flow of traffic.

Then, just as a jaded ol' grouch begins to wonder if an old friend's observation that "people are no damned good" might be true, a kind act from some delightful person contradicts the theory. Usually, the kindness comes as a total surprise and carries no expectation of reward – except for the warm feeling that envelopes donors and beneficiaries alike.

Just last Saturday, I grumbled at a driver who hurriedly ran a stop sign so he could drive slowly in my lane, causing me to sit through a long traffic light. That's no big deal, of course; it happens all the time. This time, though, it made us later for an already late lunch at Amaya's Bar & Grill, our favorite Mexican restaurant, the same one we mentioned in "Childless With Kids."

By the time we got inside, Eugene already had chips, salsa and *dos cervezas* at our regular booth. We were greeted by a patron we'd met on earlier trips. In fact, I'd messed with his little great-nephew the last time we'd seen him. As little Caleb ran around through the tables having a grand time, I jumped at him as he ran past and gruffly demanded, "**Wha-a-a-t** are you doing?" My tone stopped him in his tracks and he stood for a moment in a quiet trance trying to figure me out. Then he sought the protection of mama's skirts for a few minutes before deciding the funny old codger was only playing. Still, he moved at a slower, more cautious pace the rest of the day, checking over his shoulder from time to time to be sure of my location.

Rex Cole, the proud great-uncle, told his tablemate about me scaring the little scutter before we headed for our cervezas and chips. The rest of his family sat at the long table across the aisle and he rejoined them after his smoke. His family group varies from week to week, but it includes all age groups from toddlers to teenagers to adults to folks of the elder persuasion – like me. Rex was always there, as was his mother Shirley Stringfield, the one we identified as the matriarch before we'd ever met them.

The group had a good time, as patrons of Amaya's are prone to do, while we devoted our full attention to Bettie's number four on the lunch (beef burrito with *queso*, Mexican potatoes and *charro* beans) and one of my favorite dishes, a Chicken Enchilada dinner.

Shirley Stringfield and her son Rex Cole enjoy their Saturday lunches at Amaya's Bar & Grill

As we ate, I watched a soccer game on the TV usually tuned to a Spanish channel in the bar area. Other than speaking to Shirley once as she walked past to visit the facilities, we had no further conversations with the group. We visited with Brenda Quiroz, the young hostess and another of Estella's nieces, and joked with Eugene, the young waiter we've known since he was a teenager.

Finally, after we'd consumed everything on the table, we continued our talk with Brenda until Bettie began to fidget and look around for Eugene and our bill. Finally, Brenda smiled and said, "Your bill has already been taken care of."

"Somebody paid our bill for us! Who?" I asked as I quickly glanced around the restaurant.

"It was that lady over there," she smiled, pointing toward Mrs. Stringfield.

I walked to the table and asked, "To whom do I owe my thanks for our meal – and why? We appreciate the gesture, but how did you pick us."

"She paid it," Rex said, pointing to his mother. "We just do that every once in a while. It makes people feel good and it makes us feel good. It's fun to see the looks on their faces when you do something nice for them. We look at it as paying it forward. So, pay it forward."

I've heard all my life that giving is more rewarding than receiving. I can tell you that any favor I ever did for anyone was repaid ten times over. And, the smiles around Mrs. Stringfield's table last Saturday indicated that giving is, indeed, fun.

I can hardly wait to pay it forward and make another family happy.

WHERE WERE YOU WHEN...

Anytime a sentence begins with the phrase above, some folks recall vivid details, others either don't remember or don't care and still others mention other, equally memorable events.

I don't remember the bombing of Pearl Harbor, one of the most memorable events of my lifetime, because I was still a few months shy of my second birthday. I don't remember the exact moments that VE Day (Victory in Europe) and VJ Day (Victory in Japan) in 1945, but that was the year we moved into Aunt Vic's little house near Bishop Cemetery, so I know where I was. I remember folks talking excitedly about the war being over and my Mama and Papa's excitement over my Uncle Haskell coming home from the Navy and Uncle Lloyd getting out of the Army.

Lloyd Gresham got out of the Army after meeting his big brother Haskell Gresham in Paris before he got out of the Navy. Both my uncles got home before I started first grade.

I also remember it as the end of ration stamps. For us kids, it was the equivalent of today's pre-schoolers receiving sheets of stickers to decorate their bodies, clothing, homes. The useless ration stamps became inexpensive toys that joined our collection of pots and pans, jar lids, brown grocery sacks and wooden spoons. Who needed drums to set the beat?

I remember the day Babe Ruth died on August 16, 1948 at age 53, but I didn't hear about it the same day. We lived on and sharecropped Osto Bustle's farm by that time and the Ft. Worth Star-Telegram arrived via the U.S. mail at least a day late. Rural Free Delivery (RFD) was faster than the Pony Express, but not enough to brag about. The newspapers didn't have any arrow punctures, though, so that was a plus!

Anyhow, there was the Bambino's picture right there on the front page in his Yankee uniform. I remember another photo of a sick Babe Ruth in his pajamas sitting on the edge of his hospital bed. Although I was a dyed-in-the-wool Brooklyn Dodger fan, I was saddened by the death of the greatest hitter of all time. Too old to play for the despicable Yankees by then, he was no threat to my beloved Dodgers.

Where were you when the Korean War began and ended? Oops, two goofs in one question; it was a police action, not a war – and it ended in an uneasy truce with no winner. I was a 10-year-old kid on the Bustle Farm when it began on June 25, 1950, but I had been yanked off to the big city of Mineral Wells by the time it ended (?) in July of 1953. I had too many assimilation problems at that time to worry about some far away police action.

The next major event in my lifetime is another story altogether. I remember exactly where I was and what I was doing at 12:45 on November 22, 1963. I was sitting at my drafting board next to the aisle on the second floor of Continental Electronics Mfg. Co. I had just finished my baloney and cheese sandwich at the end of our lunch period when John Ronan screamed past. "They killed him!" he wailed. "The sonuvabitches killed him! They killed the President!"

Ronan's father was a big Democrat supporter and Kennedy stalwart. John was particularly proud of his father's recent visit with Kennedy where he picked up embossed napkins and matchbooks from Air Force One for his son to show off. To say that Ronan was devastated would be an enormous understatement. There was no one unhappier in Dallas that day.

Where were you when Reagan sent U.S. bombers after Kaddafi on April 15, 1986? I was on the island of Cyprus unaware of any outside news – until we passed several new anti-aircraft bunkers thrown up overnight and saw infantry marching in double time as if they were late for breakfast. We soon learned of the bomber strike on Libya, just a couple of stone throws across the Mediterranean.

Since the U.S. bombers had flown directly from RAF Lakenheath in the U.K., the RAF lads in Cyprus were afraid they might be an easy target for retribution. The antenna field we were assessing lay only a couple of miles from the RAF facility, but we went through a couple of new checkpoints on the way out that morning.

When we arrived, we were told to park across the road from the site and undergo a complete auto search, including the engine housing, the boot (that's British for trunk) and the undercarriage. Then we spent the day in a blacked out building. Instead of a standard trip to the RAF field for our departure the next day, we were taken to an open field where they emptied our luggage. They looked inside my camera lenses and removed the batteries in case they might be intended for bomb ignition. Then one bus carried us to the airport while a separate vehicle delivered our luggage. After a full body search, we were glad to finally get aboard the military aircraft, even if everyone did have to ride backward. They were almost as paranoid at London's Gatwick when we left England a few days later, but I don't mind safety searches – unless they're administered by males.

Where were you when O.J. Simpson was found not guilty? I don't remember where I was; I just remember my disgust. My old friend Rodney Nall, though, remembers exactly where he was. "I heard the verdict when I was in a dentist's chair getting a root canal," Nall reported. "I wasn't excited about either experience."

Where were you when the Vietnam War ended? Better yet, when did it end? Was it when the last U.S. Marine was killed? Or when Case-Church officially ended it? Those dates didn't matter much to me, but two other dates did. Capt. John S. Murphy flew his 224th

bombing mission on June 8, 1972, but he didn't return from that mission until March 27, 1973, two days before the last of the 591 American POWs got here. The intervening 9 months and 17 days were spent in horrible prison camp conditions I'm sure the rest of us can't imagine.

I had put on a metal POW bracelet with Johnny's name on it as soon as Mom told me my classmate (and her boss's son) had been shot down. The bracelet reminded me to pray for Johnny's safekeeping until that wonderful day I sent that worn, shiny piece of metal back to Johnny. That's the day Vietnam ended for me, but I still thank God every day for Capt. John S. Murphy and men like him.

Where were you when Timothy McVeigh and Terry Nichols blew up the Murrah Federal Building in Oklahoma City on April 19, 1995? I was designing trailer-mounted frequency converters for Unitron, Inc. in Garland when the fertilizer exploded. I remember employees gathered around listening to the early radio reports, then talking among themselves until more radio reports at the next break. Hearing about the 168 deaths was terrible, but knowing that 19 of them were under the age of six was heartbreaking. We had no idea that another attack in the future would kill almost 20 times as many.

You remember that day, September 11, 2001, but do you remember where you were when the planes hit the twin towers? I was sitting at a computer at Currency Systems International in Irving, Texas, when I heard the first scream. I don't remember which young lady sounded the alarm, but almost every employee found access to a TV within a couple of minutes. In retrospect, it's hard to separate which scenes I watched live and which ones I saw in later newscasts, not that it matters much; it was a gut-wrenching time for America.

I was on a big project with an impending delivery date that caused a number of us to accept second-hand reports from co-workers as we kept our eyes glued to computer screens. So, it was the end of the long day as I nosed my truck toward home that the full impact of the tragedy hit me. Unbidden tears almost caused me to pull off the freeway, but a switch to a music channel helped me get home; once there, constant replays made it worse. We must never let that happen again!

Despite civil liberties lawyers ranting against racial profiling, please remember that freckle-faced redheads haven't crashed any planes into buildings or bombed U.S. citizens. Now, I don't recommend harassing everyone who looks like the 19 fellows who hit us on 9-11, but I don't think polite inspections are racist; they're common sense. Having grown up in an era of endless clichés, I'll use another: Better safe than sorry.

I OWE YOU, RALPH

On a drive I shared with Ralph Manns to the 1986 Outdoor Writers Association of America Annual Conference in Harrisburg, Pennsylvania, I agreed to a post-conference trip to Washington, DC with my co-pilot if he agreed to visit the Beretta Gun Club in Accokeek, Maryland. At the time, it was one of only two sporting clay courses in the nation – that I knew of. I needed photos to take back to the Directors of the Dallas Gun Club who were considering the addition of sporting clays at their club. I also wanted to shoot the new sport for the first time.

I really didn't want to fight Washington traffic to see the sights, but Manns, a fisheries biologist at that time, was Major Ralph Manns during the Vietnam War. Manns served as an intelligence officer in Saigon and he insisted on a visit to the Vietnam Veterans Memorial, better known as The Wall. A close friend of his had flown off in an observation aircraft one day and never returned.

"I was the last family friend to see him alive," Manns related. "He went to visit Ruth in Hawaii on R&R. On his way back to Nam he slept on a mattress on the floor of my bullet pock-marked room in the old MACV headquarters that had been overrun by the VC during the 1968 Tet offensive. A few days later he was MIA. That status remained for ten years. Eventually he was declared KIA and his wife Ruth was able to go on with her life. A few years after the Vietnamese from the North successfully invaded the South, Carl's plane was found, apparently shot down by ground-fire. He remains the finest man I have known."

This minute section holds the name of Ralph Manns' friend, Carl F. Karst, the man whose death brought me to The Wall.

OK, I saw the Lincoln Memorial and the Washington Monument and it was nice to see things up close and personal that I had seen all my life in books, photos and movies. It's impressive, to say the least, but I never expected The Wall to affect me the way it did.

I got a late start; Manns was already walking along searching for names while I searched the location records for the exact panel that held the name of Manns' friend. I also got several sheets of paper for Manns to make shadings of the name for himself and for his friend's family. Everything was hunky-dory as long as I had projects to keep my mind busy. Once we'd located the name and Manns worked on his shadings, though, I stood to scan the length of the Wall in both directions.

Suddenly, those big, black panels full of names stunned me. It's easy to speak the number 58,000 and to write 58,000, but those panels finally hammered the magnitude of that war into my hard head. It wasn't just five little digits any more, but line after line after line of names, each of which represents a man who gave his life for our country.

A wide-angle view of the Vietnam Wall. My friend Ralph Manns is far down the wall searching for his friend's name.

A chill spread through my body as I stood before those names. Then I watched an older lady standing with her hand on the wall quietly weeping. Then I saw a man sniffling as he rubbed black onto paper over a name and realized it was Ralph. I noticed a small piece of paper held down by a small rock at the base of the wall and bent to examine it. It began, "Dear Daddy," and that's when I lost my composure.

I stopped from time to time to read a few names, but I spent most of the rest of my visit looking at mementoes left by family members and at the faces of those obviously still grieving parents, spouses and children. That's when the real cost of the Vietnam War became clear to me. It wasn't just the 58,272 soldiers now listed on the Wall, nor was it the thousands and thousands of wounded warriors. The cost of the Vietnam War includes those who waited at home for loved ones who will never return – and those who returned without their friends.

There just ain't a Wall big enough to list all the folks it hurt.

If you haven't visited the Wall, you're missing an unforgettable experience. If you have visited the Wall and saw those grieving family members or read those wonderful notes without shedding any tears yourself, you're either a tough SOB or you haven't got a heart. And if my buddy hadn't been so insistent, I probably never would have seen it for myself.

I owe you, Ralph…

Ralph Manns, left, with Major Robert Manns after the ceremony Maj. Manns attended where Robert was awarded a Silver Star for his actions over Laos. Happily, both brothers survived the war, but, sadly, they came home without friends whose names now appear on The Wall.
(Photo courtesy of Ralph Manns)

YOUTH IS WASTED ON THE YOUNG

All you old timers out there know the title above is a myth, don't you? Of course, it is! Youth is **not** wasted on the young; one **must** be young to do most of the fun things you remember. If you were older, you'd be too smart to do things that might hurt you. Just think how many great memories that would cost you.

Granted, older folks are better able to afford expensive jaunts since they've already taken care of most life requirements. Most already own their homes outright, their cars are paid for and the kids are out of college. You don't need expensive clothes to look good for a boss you don't have, or need, nor do you need expensive fuel to drive to a job you don't have; and vehicles last much longer when you eliminate that long drive to work every day.

When I was a younger, dumber whippersnapper, old timers stayed near the wood stove in the tin hunters cabin one cold morning. Sleet peppered the tin roof and wind howled through the cracks. We had none of the magic Arctic wear available today; it was blue jean jackets and wool shirts, mostly. We had heavier jackets, but it was hard to use a rifle wearing too much clothing.

A couple of us young sprouts doubted we would kill any deer in the cabin, so we donned coveralls, gloves and used our caps to hold plastic bread sacks in place. The plastic hung down our backs to keep sleet from falling into our upturned collars. I made it to the Y without freezing, but the wind was worse when I reached the ridge that ran toward the turn-around.

I had little chance of success with every step on the sleet, no matter how soft, crunching loudly enough to alarm every animal in Llano County. If I'd been older and wealthier, there's no doubt I'd have been somewhere dry and warm – and I would have missed seeing that yearling doe's effort to sneak away after I'd passed her hidey hole. The crunching of her sharp hooves on the sleet alerted me, just as my steps had warned her. I almost laughed out loud as she minced along, head down, trying to sneak past, seeming to wince at each footfall. I could almost picture the dialog balloons above her head saying, "Eww, eww, eww," every time she gingerly put a hoof down.

If I hadn't been younger, dumber and less solvent, I also would have missed some great fishing experiences. I remember being so cold one day far up the river channel at Lake o' the Pines that Clinton Metcalf and I pulled into a protected cove for a midafternoon nap. The only way to get warm was to lie in the bottom of the boat out of the wind and soak up what sun there was. But we were enjoying one of God's finest creations; that old river channel is a favorite video I watch on the back of my eyelids.

My older self certainly wouldn't have launched my old Top Tenner bass boat in Cutoff Lake near Trinidad that January day. My brother-in-law Billy Hamilton and I launched before daybreak, well before the little store at the boat ramp opened. We both wore insulated gear, topped with lined ski masks and heavy caps. As we slowly worked the river bends with worms and jigs, we had to swish our rod tips in the water to melt ice in our eyelets after every retrieve.

When moving to a new area with the big motor, we found that high speed runs hurt less than slower runs that exposed us to less wind, but for a longer period. By 10:00 AM, after we'd had all the fun we could stand, we were stunned to read 6° F on the thermometer at the store where we paid our launching fee. The storekeeper said it had been 0° at sunup. Dang! Channel 5's Harold Taft had promised us it would only drop to 23° or so. Oh, well, the heater in my truck worked well on the nice drive home.

In my youth, I remember leaving camp with temperatures in the 30s wearing nothing more than long johns under my jeans and flannel shirt topped with what would be called a light jacket today. Then I climbed up a tree and sat on a cross board for several hours. If it was really cold, I'd pick a suitable tree and lean against the trunk to stay out of the wind.

By the time I dropped off my last deer lease, I was wearing layer after layer of Arctic clothing, including boots, hat and ski mask, just to ride my ATV out to a heated blind. Frankly, I preferred the rough conditions of those early days, but old joints ache far too badly to endure it in the name of fun. But would I take youth now in exchange for not having it as a youngster? Nah, I enjoyed my youth – all the way through last week…

Today I ran across my handwritten copy of the valedictory address I wrote and presented in May of 1958 at Mineral Wells High School. Surprisingly enough, it would be just as appropriate today by adding Islamic terrorists to our list of enemies. Bear in mind that I was a mere child of 18 when I wrote this and it was extremely difficult for me to ignore my sometimes awkward text – but using editing abilities honed over the 56 years since then would be cheating, now wouldn't it?

WAKE UP AMERICA!

Millions of Americans are understandably alarmed when they look out upon the international scene. Whatever our hopes may be, we are confronted by the possibility that war may overtake us. There is a general demand that we not only maintain a lead in defense weapons, but also that we prevent infiltration by our arch enemy, communism, in order that it may not exert an appalling influence upon American thinking and the formation of our national policies. In the face of actual danger, the public is genuinely concerned about the general welfare.

The deadliest enemies of nations are not their foreign foes, but those that dwell within their borders, and from these internal enemies civilization is always in need of being saved. The nation blessed above all nations is she whose people do the saving day by day by speaking, writing and voting reasonably. People attain these qualities through our educational process.

It is the fundamental purpose of education to develop as fully as possible the range of this mysterious and amazing human capacity of directing our interests according to our own states of mind, our beliefs and our ideals. Deprive a man of these capacities and education will become meaningless – indeed, impossible!

If the development of the human capacity for reflection is the essence of education and, consequently, the essential task of educational institutions, the mere accumulation of knowledge is not education.

The first goal of education is to develop the power to distinguish what is first rate. The mark of an educated man is his sense of values.

Our destiny, then, depends upon our choices, and our character is determined by what we choose. Since young people are called upon to make the most important decisions, we are now living the most important time of our lives.

Our choice is not only between good and bad, or between black and white. Sometimes it is between shades of gray, or between good and better. Unfortunately, many of our choices are hastily made because of other matters we consider more important. We are so busy that we leave the finest values outside our lives because we are cluttered with so many trivial things.

A challenge to parents and teachers, as well as the students, is to prevent these hasty, ill formed opinions. Adults should take the lead in assisting students in choosing the courses in their curriculum. The more gifted children should be stimulated so that they will accomplish their greatest possible achievements.

The process of education is that knowledge may expand and increase. For these and other reasons we may look forward to a future in which the creative powers of the human mind are used in the service of mankind to a degree never before known.

Most of our educational problems are due to the fact that we let others do our thinking for us; we accept ready-made opinions instead of thinking things through; we permit ourselves to be spoon-fed our ideas and convictions by press and radio rather than take the trouble to acquire them for ourselves. The result is that while we pride ourselves on being highly educated, we are victims of propaganda, our minds accept completely contradictory conclusions, and our national policies are aimed in several directions at the same time.

There has been more concern with, and thinking about, education on the part of American citizens during current years than there has been for decades. This concern is inevitably accompanied by controversy, for conflicts of ideas are inevitable in decision making. Creative and farsighted decisions as to the role of education in the nation's life must now be made by the American people.

The education we need is the kind that will free creative abilities while, at the same time, it instills in men a sobering sense of the responsibility they carry, individually and collectively, in the formidable task of building a better world than men have yet dreamed of.

Education is the weapon which must make our nation secure. Education is the valuable weapon of defense not only against natural enemies, but against those within who, because of ignorance, prejudice and fear, would tear down our heritage.

Education is a process to which mankind is submitted, consciously or unconsciously, throughout life. It begins in the cradle and death finds it still uncompleted. Education is not something that is done to one formally with the aid of teachers and books alone, but it is rather the result of one's own reaction to outside stimuli. The educated man or woman is the traveler who walks along life's highway with observant eyes. No matter which path he may choose, if he perceives and gives thought to the stimuli which touch him on every side, he is an educated man.

1958 Salutatorian Gail Hughes, left,
and the ecstatic valedictorian

(Photo by Karen Hamilton, 2014)

About the author: Morris Gresham enjoyed simultaneous careers. He began in the mechanical design field in 1960 and worked through several design and management engineering positions until his retirement as a senior mechanical engineer in 2002.

He currently is a freelance writer living in Ovilla, Texas. He began hunting and fishing during his youth on an Erath County, Texas farm during the 1940s. He began his writing career in 1974 and has since published hundreds of magazine articles in dozens of national, regional and state publications. He has been published in *Sports Afield*, *Outdoor Life*, *Bassmaster Magazine*, *Texas Fisherman*, *Texas Fish & Game Magazine*, *Texas Trophy Hunters Magazine*, *Texas Parks & Wildlife Magazine*, *Texas Sportsman Magazine*, *The In-Fisherman* and many others.

Gresham was the Outdoors columnist for the DeSoto, Texas *Focus Daily News* in 2002-2003 and won a national writing competition for one of those columns. He was a columnist for *The Skeet Shooting Review*, a national publication, from August, 1996 until his retirement in January, 2009, winning another national competition for one of those columns. He served as the *Skeet Shooting Review's* World Championships of Skeet reporter for nine years. Gresham served as editor of *USA Outdoors*, a national publication, in 1985. He edited other publications, among them, *Our Inland Fisheries*, *Bass Clubber Magazine* and *The Texas Lake Atlas*. Since Gresham's retirement from magazine and newspaper writing, he published four books, including this one. They are, in order, A *COUNTRY BOY'S APPETITE, COMING UP A COUNTRY BOY, THEN THE COUNTRY BOY WROTE...* and *SNIPPETS FROM A COUNTRY BOY'S MIND.*

Made in the USA
San Bernardino, CA
20 February 2015